PROGRESS THROUGH LENT

PROGRESS THROUGH LENT

A course for pilgrims

by
GEORGE BENNET

Foreword by
PETER NOTT
Bishop of Norwich

The Canterbury Press
Norwich

First published 1993 by The Canterbury Press Norwich
(a publishing imprint of Hymns Ancient & Modern Limited,
a registered charity)
St Mary's Works, St Mary's Plain,
Norwich, Norfolk, NR3 3BH

British Library Cataloguing in Publication Data

A catalogue record for this book is available
from the British Library

ISBN 1-85311-065-5

*Typeset by Datix International Limited
Bungay, Suffolk and
Printed and bound in Great Britain by
St Edmundsbury Press Limited
Bury St Edmunds, Suffolk*

Foreword

by the Rt Revd Peter Nott
Bishop of Norwich

Pilgrimage is an important concept for Christians for we are, like our Jewish forefathers, a pilgrim people for whom life is a journey towards the Kingdom of God. As part of this journey, many of us make little pilgrimages from time to time to holy places. In this part of England, thousands of people every year come to visit our fine Cathedral, the Shrine of our Lady at Walsingham, the cell of Mother Julian, and our unique heritage of medieval churches.

Our pilgrimage can also be an inner journey – a pilgrimage of prayer in the company of Christ, who accompanies us on every step through life's journey. This Lent Book written by a priest who, until his recent retirement served with me in this diocese, provides us with just such an opportunity. It guides us on a pilgrimage we can undertake in our own homes either alone or which we can share with the many others who will be reading this book with us. It offers a most helpful way of listening to the Word of God and reflecting on its meaning for our own pilgrimage.

It is a challenging book as well as an encouraging one, because a pilgrimage should inspire us not only to reflection, but to action. My hope is that this book will enable all who read it to fulfil a prayer I always associate with Lent . . .

> O Most Merciful Redeemer, Friend and Brother,
> May I know thee more clearly,
> Love thee more dearly,
> And follow thee more nearly,
> day by day.

+ Peter Norvic

Contents

Preface

The effort of a Christian during Lent is essentially a solitary one. It is therefore well-suited to being based on a book. I have noticed that many people who do not often read books (let alone Christian books) are prepared to work through a book in Lent, particularly if it comes divided up into short sections, a day at a time. Serious Christians expect to be challenged during Lent, and they expect what they read to be strong, Jesus-centred, and practical.

Much of the material in this book originated in actual pastoral situations in the parish. I have adapted it for a wider audience; but I hope it retains something of the freshness of teaching and ministry in the real parish situation.

The introductory section covers the three weeks leading into Lent; there is a preparatory double-page for each of these three weeks. But from Ash Wednesday there is a double-page for each day through Lent. The appropriate scripture passages are printed in the text – a help, I hope, for busy people. The Bible version used is the New International Version (NIV).

Lent must be a solitary effort, but it cannot be a selfish one. Its effect should subsequently show in the increased warmth and vitality of the whole church community. Some churches, with this in mind, like to arrange weekly discussion groups in the parish, so at the end of each section I have provided a few Discussion Starters. Although the book is written for Church of England readers – and I seek to draw from the full scope of its Catholic and Evangelical traditions – I believe Methodists, Roman Catholics and others will be quite at home with it too. I assume a serious Christian will be in church every Sunday during Lent, as well as on Ash Wednesday and at the key moments of Holy Week. I have mostly avoided overlap with the readings of *The Alternative Service Book 1980* lectionary, at least until later in Lent when the focus narrows inevitably on the Passion of our Lord.

My thanks are due to the congregations I have served over the years, whose needs at various times originally prompted many of these writings, and whose fellowship in the defence and confirmation of the Gospel have been of more value to me than I could ever find words to express.

Wymondham 1992   GEORGE BENNET

How to use this book

It is a most wholesome tradition of the Church to spend the six weeks of Lent seeking to strengthen our Christian lives and deepen our faith. I want to help you make a determined attempt this Lent to walk closer with the Lord and to know him better.

For Jesus the six weeks following his baptism in the River Jordan was a solitary time; and this has always been the model for the Christian. For him it was a time to consider the path he would tread and the methods he would follow. It was a time to reject the False, and embrace the True, whatever the cost. I assume you have a similar seriousness of purpose.

Many Christians like to be part of a discussion group once a week during Lent. It can be a stimulus and a help. The *Discussion Starters* at the ends of the chapters are intended to help such groups get going. But the essential part is the daily time you spend on your own, thinking and praying through that day's passage.

If you are reading this, you probably claim to be a Christian, or at least a Christian by intention. But who am I writing for?

Christians who have gone stale

Church-goers in a rut

People overwhelmed with doubt

Prodigal children on their way back

Seekers for Truth wherever it leads

As well as ordinary Church people who have always taken Lent seriously and mean to do so again. In short, I have in mind all for whom Christ gave his life to bring us new and abundant life. You should not wait for the start of Lent before you consider how you will spend it. Make use of the section covering the three preparatory weeks, so that you are ready, staff in hand, when your Lenten pilgrimage begins on Ash Wednesday.

My plea is that you put into practice what you learn. In the course of Lent I touch on many areas of Christian doctrine, and I hope this strengthens your understanding of the Faith. But my primary concern is that you see their implications for your life. The Kingdom is not for the intellectual, but for the obedient; it is for those who are prepared to be led into a childlike faith in our loving heavenly Father and in the Saviour he has given us.

May the Lord be with you on your journey!

The Weeks Leading into Lent: Preparing for the Journey

SETTING OBJECTIVES

Almighty God, in whom we live and move and have our being, who made us for yourself, so that our hearts are restless till they rest in you: grant us purity of heart and strength of purpose, that no selfish passion may hinder us from knowing your will, no weakness from doing it; but that in your light me may see light clearly, and in your service find our perfect freedom; through Jesus Christ our Lord.

St Augustine of Hippo
5th Century

A light to see by

> When Jesus spoke again to the people, he said: 'I am the light of the world. Whoever follows me will never walk in darkness, but will have the light of life.' JOHN 8:12

What did Jesus mean when he talked about light – or for that matter when he spoke of darkness? He seems to be telling us that without him we are like a man stumbling round a dark room, bruising himself on corners, and damaging both himself and the furniture. If only there was light to see by! The trouble with darkness is that you do not know what it contains. Imagination fills the room with nameless obstacles and dangers, and you do not know what you are up against. Then you reach the light switch, and you laugh; for now the room looks just as it always did. But in the dark it was not like that.

Near the start of *Pilgrims Progress* Bunyan describes a man being shown the path he should take.

> *'Do you see yonder shining light?' He said, 'I think I do.' Then said Evangelist, 'Keep that light in your eye, and go up directly thereto.'*

Our Lord Jesus Christ is that light. Only someone from outside this poor old world could possibly shine as a light in it. Anything else is just a repeat of what we have seen before. But Jesus Christ came from outside and spoke and acted as no man had ever done before. In him those early disciples found a light to see by; having met him they no longer needed to go fumbling and bungling their way through life.

20th Century Darkness

Modern Man is in the dark and has lost his way. He has pinned his hopes on a scientific revolution, but finds himself in danger of destroying his own planet with bombs and pollution and economic chaos. He is puzzled. He sees suffering as a scandal. Death laughs at his best efforts. And as for *life* – he doubts whether it has any meaning at all.

But Modern Man, for all his scientific ways, has chosen to ignore one vital piece of evidence – a thing no scientist should dare to do. For

Modern Man ignores the fact of Jesus Christ. Small wonder he is puzzled, as he strives to create a fantasy world of his own imagining, without Christ.

Modern Man says: 'Life is just a product of genes, environment, random variations and evolution. I am not responsible for what I am or how I behave. We are on our own in this Universe. This life is all there is. When I die, that's the end.' Modern Man has eyes only for the physical setting of his life. He refuses to notice the solid spiritual bedrock on which it all rests. Seeing only part of reality, he comes to the conclusion that life is precarious and insecure. He is like a short-sighted person looking at one of those great steel television masts. Not able to focus on the guy-ropes stretching out in all directions he wonders how the mast manages to stay balanced on such a small base. But let him put on his spectacles, and he will see how secure it is!

The lens you need is the life and death of Jesus Christ. You must fall into step with him, and learn to see things his way. The Universe is not a meaningless pattern in his eyes.

Jesus Christ claimed to come from outside, from the presence of the Creator of it all. He demonstrated in his life and death the power and love of God, and claimed to be the source of all true life – of which biological life is just the shadow. He held us responsible for our sins, but died to save us from them. Finally he rose to a new and glorious life – a life he promised to share with all who place their faith in him.

Do you see yonder shining light? If you think you do, even ever so dimly, then keep that light in your eye these coming weeks. There is light enough in our Lord Jesus Christ for you too. The Light is not really in the distance; it only seems so at first.

8th Week before Easter

The desert experience

> And the Levites said: 'Stand up and praise the Lord your God, who is from everlasting to everlasting.'
>
> 'Blessed be your glorious name.... You alone are the Lord.... You give life to everything, and the multitudes of heaven worship you. You saw the suffering of our forefathers in Egypt; you heard their cry at the Red Sea.... You divided the sea before them, so that they passed through it on dry ground.... You came down on Mount Sinai; you spoke to them from heaven. You gave them regulations and laws that are just and right, and decrees and commands that are good. You made known to them your holy Sabbath and gave them commands, decrees and laws through your servant Moses....
>
> 'Because of your great compassion you did not abandon them in the desert. By day the pillar of cloud did not cease to guide them on their path, nor the pillar of fire by night to shine on the way they were to take. You gave your good Spirit to instruct them. You did not withhold your manna from their mouths, and you gave them water for their thirst.   NEHEMIAH 9:5–20

The desert has always drawn the People of God. Jesus was not the first or the last to feel the need to go out into the wilderness to be alone with God. The hermits of early Christian centuries went out into the desert in their search for God and for Truth.

The formative experience of the Jewish people was the desert journey under Moses from Egypt to the Promised Land; here they started to learn how to be God's people. Let us think about that wilderness journey for a moment, and try to relate to it. Can it teach us how to be serious in our pilgrimage through Lent?

A new life-style

God was laying out for the Jews a completely new way of living. Every area of life was affected. We are not obliged to follow their life-style (though the Ten Commandments remain fundamental); we have not come to Mount Sinai, but *to Jesus the mediator of a new covenant* (Hebrews 12:24). In the light of Christ you must be prepared for a re-adjustment of your life-style – if you are serious.

New religious practices

For the People of Israel everything was new; there were new patterns of worship; new ways of approaching God; new ways of finding forgiveness; new ways of dedicating their lives in his service, and so on. For us the ways of approaching God are provided through Christ. The Church calls these the *means of grace:*

The Eucharist (Holy Communion); the Word of God (The Bible); Prayer (alone and with others); the Fellowship of the Church; the Reconciling Ministry of the Church; and the giving of ourselves and our money in good works.

Alongside using this book, you should make use of the means of grace God has provided. All Christians do, though we have a tendency to pick and choose. But they are meant as a complete package, and most of us need to widen our Christian experience. If for you the Eucharist is the all-important ingredient, then this Lent you should try to find Christ also in the Bible. If you are one for whom the daily Bible reading is the vital thing, then seek also the living touch of Christ in the Holy Communion. Discuss with your Parish Priest about making a confession, if you have never done so; in any case be much, MUCH more serious about examining your life and bringing your sins and failures to God. Re-assess your prayer life, and your giving of time and money in God's service. Seek, this Lent, a more balanced Christian life and a new maturity in Christ.

New ways of guidance

The cloud over the Israelite camp was there to guide them. When the cloud moved they were to follow; when it stopped they were to stay put. The cloud was a reminder of the presence of God among them: *My Presence will go with you, and I will give you rest.* (Exodus 33:14). We have no visible cloud but the word of Jesus: *I will be with you always, to the very end of the age.* (Matthew 28:20).

He would like to guide you on your journey. This Lent you should consider what he is saying to you. Perhaps the cloud moved on for you some time ago, and you never noticed! Perhaps it rests, and you have been hankering to move on. The Lord can guide us if we are prepared to follow. We only need to give him time to speak to us. This Lent can be such a time.

7th Week before Easter

The Royal Bridegroom

> Jesus said: 'All things have been committed to me by my Father. No one knows the Son except the Father, and no one knows the Father except the Son and those to whom the Son chooses to reveal him.
>
> 'Come to me, all you who are weary and burdened, and I will give you rest. Take my yoke upon you and learn from me, for I am gentle and humble in heart, and you will find rest for your souls. For my yoke is easy and my burden is light.' MATTHEW 11:27–30

To be a serious Christian means receiving the yoke that binds us to Christ in a life-long partnership. This is the part that many find hard to accept. It is one thing to come to Christ to gain help and strength for our lives. It is another to bow the head and accept his yoke. So much of our energy in every-day living is spent asserting our own identity and independence. And here is Jesus inviting us to forfeit that independence, and accept a new identity in partnership with himself.

We do such a thing willingly enough when we enter into marriage, but there the partnership is an equal one. In this yoking to Jesus we know that he must always be the senior partner. To accept the yoke of Christ means sacrificing our independence – and we resist it. We would like the help of Jesus in our daily lives, as long as he does not get too close to us. We would like him as our Saviour, but not as our Lord.

But we are asking an impossibility. The story of Man from the garden of Eden onwards is his attempt to be independent of his God. The whole work of the Saviour is to put that story into reverse, and bring us back into fellowship with our God and the dependence on him for which we were created. If you come to Christ, you must accept his yoke of obedience. What we need saving from above all else is our desire to be independent. There is no other salvation available. The Great Physician has made his diagnosis and prescribed his treatment – and the essential part of it is taking his yoke.

In a marriage the sharing of little things, myriads of them, are the magic of a developing close relationship. It is such a relationship that our Lord Jesus Christ offers his friends. Indeed we are invited to see marriage as the ideal illustration of the relationship between Christ

6

and the Christian. *Marriage signifies the mystical union that is betwixt Christ and his Church,* says the old marriage service. Or, in the new service: *It is God's purpose that husband and wife should be united in love as Christ is united with his Church.*

But how distant is the friendship most of us have with the Lord. A formal good morning, a nod before bed, this is all we share – until the big crises are upon us. Little things make a marriage; and it is the little things Jesus would have us share with him, not only the great storms of life.

For this reason a man will leave his father and mother and be united to his wife, and the two will become one flesh, quotes our Lord from the book of Genesis (2:24). Unfortunately in some marriages this growing unity that God intends never really happens. There is no real sharing in the small things, and so none at deeper levels. In the same way some Christians belong to Christ in name only. There is no everyday sharing, no continual loving in small things, and the relationship gradually becomes a burden and a meaningless chore of religious activities.

So come afresh to our Lord Jesus Christ. Accept his yoke; and in that partnership allow him to reveal to you new depths of the boundless love of God. He is the matchless Bridegroom, knowing well how to call forth renewed love in the hardest heart, able to kindle the warmth of true affection if there is any spark of love still left. He knows how to form the silver in our relationship with him, and in the fullness of time even how to touch it with gold.

Ash Wednesday – the start of Lent

Prepared for the Lord

> A voice of one calling in the desert,
> Prepare the way for the Lord,
> make straight paths for him. . . .

John said to the crowds coming out to be baptised by him, 'You brood of vipers! Who warned you to flee from the coming wrath? Produce fruit in keeping with repentance. And do not begin to say to yourselves, "We have Abraham as our father." For I tell you that out of these stones God can raise up children for Abraham. The axe is already at the root of the trees, and every tree that does not produce good fruit will be cut down and thrown into the fire.'

'What should we do then?' the crowd asked. John answered, 'The man with two tunics should share with him who has none, and the one who has food should do the same.'

Tax collectors also came to be baptised. 'Teacher,' they asked, 'what should we do?' 'Don't collect any more than you are required to,' he told them.

Then some soldiers asked him, 'And what should we do?' He replied, 'Don't extort money and don't accuse people falsely – be content with your pay.'

The people were waiting expectantly and were all wondering in their hearts if John might possibly be the Christ. John answered them all, 'I baptise you with water. But one more powerful than I will come, the thongs of whose sandals I am not worthy to untie. He will baptise you with the Holy Spirit and with fire.'   LUKE 3:4,7-16

In John the Baptist's day people thought of the coming of the Messiah – the Christ – in very worldly terms. They expected him to fit in with their ideas of how things ought to be done. Jesus did not fit in at all; nor does he usually fit in with the popular cultural ideas of our day.

Repentance

If the people around John were to relate to the Messiah when he came their hearts needed to be returned to see things God's way; and this was the pre-occupation of John's preaching before Jesus appeared.

This change of heart he called REPENTANCE. He was forthright in exposing the things that people needed to clear from their lives. Pharisees were to give up pretence in their religion, tax collectors were to give up dishonesty, soldiers were to give up cruel violence, and ordinary people were to give up selfishly hoarding scarce goods, and assuming that their Jewish descent made everything alright with God. We need the same sorts of change of heart – if the cap fits, wear it, as they say! And do not say, 'I am no Jew or Pharisee.' For you can say exactly the same sorts of things about being English and a member of the Church of England.

Hope

But alongside this fearless exposure of evil John made use of another weapon, HOPE. As John's mission progressed, everyone started to be on tip-toe looking for the appearing of the Messiah. Having prepared a people whose hearts were once more in tune with God, he was able to present to their vision the limitless possibilities in the coming of the Messiah, who would baptise them *with the Holy Spirit and with fire*. John could offer a baptism that spoke of a change of heart and a new attitude; and he could raise keen expectation of the Christ who was to come.

But the Messiah, John pointed out, would go further than that, and offer the inner regeneration that only the Holy Spirit can bring about. In his hands forgiveness would be no mere writing off past debts by God. It would be a creative act launching a person's life on a new path. The Lord Jesus could promise: *Blessed are those who hunger and thirst for righteousness, for they will be filled.* (Matthew 5:6) – Yes, FILLED! – the righteousness of Jesus their possession, through and through.

John had just one task left to do, to point out the Messiah to everyone who would stop and listen – the Saviour, the long-awaited Christ, promised many centuries before by God. This he did, unmistakably, the minute he appeared: *Look, the Lamb of God, who takes away the sin of the world! This is the one I meant. . . .* John 1:29–30

Thursday after Ash Wednesday

True and false disciples

> As they were walking along the road, a man said to him, 'I will follow you wherever you go.' Jesus replied, 'Foxes have holes and birds of the air have nests, but the Son of Man has no place to lay his head.'
>
> He said to another man, 'Follow me.' But the man replied, 'Lord, first let me go and bury my father.' Jesus said to him, 'Let the dead bury their own dead, but you go and proclaim the kingdom of God.'
>
> Still another said, 'I will follow you, Lord; but first let me go back and say good-bye to my family.' Jesus replied, 'No-one who puts his hand to the plough and looks back is fit for service in the kingdom of God.' LUKE 9:57–62

The Lord Jesus was gathering disciples and preparing them for his mission. Some of them had false ideas about following him. They needed to be rebuked and warned. The essential point of the story is that those rebuked seemed so very reasonable. Only the answers Jesus gave revealed the false thinking. Our Lord puts his finger unerringly on any phoney point in our commitment.

I will follow you wherever you go
You can't fault that, can you? What more could any minister ask for? And many people would go on from this commitment to a life-time of faithful service. But in *this* man's commitment Jesus sensed something was wrong. He was over-enthusiastic; it was an impulsive decision, and the cost had not been properly counted. He was imagining an endless crest-of-the-wave experience with Jesus; and he had not noticed that the road they would travel together went through places with names like Gethsemane and Calvary.

First let me go and bury my father
He is not talking about the funeral; in the Middle East that would follow the same day, and occasion only trivial delay. No, he is telling Jesus that the old man is getting a bit frail; it's a comfort for him to have his son at home. Therefore, much as he would love to serve Jesus, it must wait until his father has died.

How very reasonable! I would not dare take him to task. People often decline to help for reasons of this sort: 'When the children leave home.' – 'When I've finished this job for my friend.' I dare not query such reasons. After all, the Lord Jesus does not want us ignoring commitments to family and friends. But in *this* case he knows it is just an excuse. The man is really saying: 'Yes, Lord, but not yet.' It is a case of slow obedience being no obedience. When Jesus calls, he knows all about our circumstances. Excuses are out of place. The time to answer is *now*.

First let me say good-bye

He wants to tell his family of his new commitment. Good! But who said anything about saying goodbye? Should we break links with family and friends to follow Christ? There may be some things, even people, you will need to drop. But you came to Jesus with the family and friends he has given you; together with all the things that make up YOU – enjoyments, interests, hobbies. There is no need to say good-bye to it all.

But clearly, in *this* man's case Jesus knew the pull the family might exert. This man needed first to cement his decision to follow Christ, and establish his discipleship. Then perhaps he could explain it to his family. If not, . . . And our Lord uses that lovely picture of a ploughman at work. If his thoughts are of home, what sort of a furrow is he going to plough?

There used to be ploughing matches in the field outside my home. Actually they were called *Drawing Matches*, and the word says something about the precision achieved. The winning furrow might deviate less than an inch in two hundred yards. When you asked how they did it, they pointed to a distant tree. 'I look between the horses at that tree, and never take my eyes off it for a moment.' That is the pattern for true discipleship. We keep our eyes on the distant goal, and nothing and no one is going to distract us.

We follow one who knew how to 'plough'. From early in his public ministry his face was set resolutely towards Jerusalem – and Gethsemane and Calvary – and the glory beyond. He had measured coolly the cost of it all. He would need in the end to leave his beloved mother in the care of a friend. Family and friends would do their best to deflect him. But he kept his eye on the distant goal, and ploughed a furrow straight and true.

Friday after Ash Wednesday

Two tests

> Do not store up for yourselves treasures on earth, where moth and rust destroy, and where thieves break in and steal. But store up for yourselves treasures in heaven, where moth and rust do not destroy, and where thieves do not break in and steal. For where you treasure is, there your heart will be also. MATTHEW 6:19–21

> Watch out for false prophets. They come to you in sheep's clothing, but inwardly they are ferocious wolves. By their fruit you will recognise them. Do people pick grapes from thornbushes, or figs from thistles? Likewise every good tree bears good fruit, but a bad tree bears bad fruit. A good tree cannot bear bad fruit, and a bad tree cannot bear good fruit. Every tree that does not bear good fruit is cut down and thrown into the fire. Thus, by their fruit you will recognise them.
> MATTHEW 7:15–20

Recently the smell of boiling oranges was filling our house; for the marmalade season had arrived. In due course it was necessary to know whether the marmalade was ready to *set*. Each housewife seems to have her own test – saucers waved in the cool air by the back door, wooden spoons lifted dripping from the cauldron, scientific tests with thermometers and chemicals; and Granny just takes one look and says 'It's ready now.' Here are two tests you can apply to help you decide whether your Christian life is properly *set*.

The Treasure Test
Jesus said: *Where your treasure is, there your heart will be also*. What is your *treasure*? What is there in your life that other things must make way for? What is the activity that you will always make time for? What would you not go without in any circumstances? What is the thing on which you will always spend any spare cash? What matters most to you? In short, what is your *treasure*?

The way Jesus puts it, it is clear that we can have only one treasure. There may be many important things in our lives, things that are good and desirable and wholesome, things that our loving heavenly Father delights to shower upon us. But there can only be one thing that has top priority – only one *treasure*. What does the *Treasure Test* show you about yourself?

The Fruit Test
Jesus said: *By their fruit you will recognise them*. Never mind the false prophets for the moment; look at yourself. What *fruit* is there from your Christian life? We all seek to equip our lives with those patterns of loving, unselfish behaviour that we know our Lord desires. But the question we need to answer is whether these things grow naturally out of the inner life we share with him; or are they things hung at random on our lives to give a brave show for all to see, like the coloured baubles and lights on a Christmas tree. How do you tell the difference?

The real fruit contains the seed by which new life is spread abroad; the pretend fruit does not. The real fruit of a Christian life is used by the Holy Spirit in the work of making Christ known; the pretend fruit is not. So what you need to consider is whether the pattern of your life helps lead others nearer to Christ. When you are about, does Jesus seem more real? Do people find it hard to doubt his love when you are there? Have you ever said a word that really helped someone into faith? *I chose you to go and bear fruit – fruit that will last.* (John 15:16) What does the *Fruit Test* say about your Christian life?

And if your life does not meet these tests? . . . Why then, it is the highest joy of our blessed Lord to put it right, and to form in you a Christian life that is stable and *set*. But first your eyes must be open.

Saturday after Ash Wednesday

A good sort of fire

'See, I will send my messenger, who will prepare the way before me. Then suddenly the Lord you are seeking will come to his temple; the messenger of the covenant, whom you desire, will come,' says the Lord Almighty.

But who can endure the day of his coming? Who can stand when he appears? For he will be like a refiner's fire or a launderer's soap. He will sit as a refiner and purifier of silver; he will purify the Levites and refine them like gold and silver. Then the Lord will have men who will bring offerings in righteousness, and the offerings of Judah and Jerusalem will be acceptable to the Lord, as in days gone by, as in former years.

'They will be mine,' says the Lord Almighty, 'in the day when I make up my treasured possession. . . . And you will again see the distinction between the righteous and the wicked, between those who serve God and those who do not.   MALACHI 3:1-4; 17-18

It was a potent image for his hearers, for they had all watched the refiner of silver at work. He would sit cross-legged before a brazier on which rested his refining crucible. The raw silver was melted in this. It came to him from the mines full of impurities, a crumbling material that could not be worked, and must be refined.

In contact with the air a scum gathered on its surface as the impurities oxidised; the silver itself scarcely oxidised at all. This scum would then be scraped off and discarded, revealing a fresh bright surface of molten metal. Before long this in turn tarnished and further dross formed upon it. Again it would be scraped; and again the scum would form. But at last only the pure silver was left – silver capable of being worked into fine jewellery. The refiner would go on till he could see his own face reflected steadily in the molten surface.

Have you ever thought of the work of our Lord Jesus like this? For it is his intention to purify our lives until he can see his own face and likeness in us. But there is so much dross! Perhaps for a moment there is a glimpse of him in our lives. But then the surface darkens, and the image vanishes. With infinite patience he continues with the refining, finding new ways of exposing us to the air of the world that will most certainly reveal our hidden shortcomings. Sometimes it almost seems unfair how we are put in situations that will inevitably bring out the worst in us; but it is quite deliberate on his part.

We are not the only ones whose lives he is working to refine and purify. In the fellowship of the Church we shall meet many others who are experiencing the patient pressure of that love; our interaction with them provides much of the refining fire. They bring out both the worst and the best in us; and thus slowly we learn to reject the one and embrace the other, and to find his love in them all. His purpose is the transformation of the whole of human life until the line between righteousness and wickedness is no longer blurred in our eyes, and we discover together how wonderful is the wisdom and knowledge of our God.

We fear that refining fire, for it spells adversity and trouble. But how foolish we are, for it is all love, and all good. What a glory it will be when the work is done, and finally he can use us as a setting for his jewels.

O Lord God, when you give to your servants to endeavour any great matter, grant us also to know that it is not the beginning, but the continuing of the same, until it is thoroughly finished, which yields the true glory; through him who for the finishing of your work laid down his life, our Redeemer, Jesus Christ.

Sir Francis Drake
16th Century

Discussion Starters
– *The Weeks leading into Lent*

1. What should be the ingredients of a fully balanced Christian life? Which of the means of grace (page 5) are you missing out on?

2. Christian discipleship has been described as *freedom in obedience*, just as marriage is a bondage that gives a new sort of freedom. Can

marriage really illuminate the ideal relationship between Christ and his disciples?

3. What do you hope the Lord will do for you and your Church fellowship this Lent?

1st Week in Lent: Starting on the Road

GETTING THE FIRST STEPS RIGHT

We ask you, O God, to pour your grace into our hearts; that as at the message of an angel, Mary was overshadowed by the Holy Spirit, and became the mother of the Lord and the most blessed among women, so we, believing your word, may receive Christ to dwell in our hearts, and by our life make manifest the mystery of his incarnation; who has exalted our Manhood into the glory of his Godhead, even Jesus Christ our Lord.

The Gregorian Sacramentary
6th Century

1st Sunday in Lent

The first of miracles

> The angel said to Mary, 'You will be with child and give birth to a son, and you are to give him the name Jesus. He will be great and will be called the Son of the Most High. . . .' 'How will this be,' Mary asked the angel, 'since I am a virgin?'
>
> The angel answered, 'The Holy Spirit will come upon you, and the power of the Most High will overshadow you. So the holy one to be born will be called the Son of God. . . .'
>
> 'I am the Lord's servant,' Mary answered. 'May it be to me as you have said.'   LUKE 1:30–38

> Jesus declared, 'I tell you the truth, unless a man is born again, he cannot see the kingdom of God.' 'How can a man be born when he is old?' Nicodemus asked. 'Surely he cannot enter a second time into his mother's womb to be born!'
>
> Jesus answered, 'I tell you the truth, unless a man is born of water and the Spirit, he cannot enter the kingdom of God. Flesh gives birth to flesh, but the Spirit gives birth to spirit. You should not be surprised at my saying, "You must be born again." The wind blows wherever it pleases. You hear its sound, but you cannot tell where it comes from or where it is going. So it is with everyone born of the Spirit.'   JOHN 3:3–8

I BELIEVE in the Virgin Birth of our Lord Jesus Christ for a whole variety of reasons. To spell it out quite precisely, I believe that he had no human father, but was conceived in the womb of the Blessed Virgin Mary, his Mother, by a direct and miraculous intervention of God the Holy Spirit. I believe it because the Bible clearly says so, and because the Church has always clearly taught it, and still does. I believe it because Christians in all ages have lived holy lives and died, staking their eternal destiny on this truth and on the teaching that flows from it. It is an impressive body of evidence.

I am not impressed by the sort of pseudo-scientific reasoning that starts with the assumption, *virgin births don't happen*, and then refuses to look at the evidence. That is not scientific. Our present state of knowledge does not allow us to say how God might interact with the Universe he has created.

18

But I do find I am increasingly impressed by how fitting the Virgin Birth is. It seems so perfectly in keeping with our knowledge of the spiritual life. As a physical event it was unique, and could happen only once. But in a spiritual sense it is constantly repeated in the lives of individuals. When people first turn to the Lord, the Holy Spirit comes upon them, the power of the Most High overshadows them, and the Son of God is conceived in their hearts by faith. Just once the miracle had to happen physically; but it is endlessly repeated in the hearts and lives of people in all ages.

'But,' you say, 'did I not receive the New Birth by water and the Spirit at my baptism?' Yes, indeed! Every blessing God can shower upon us was given to us in our baptism – actually GIVEN. It is a great hamper of gifts, too many to list, with labels like FORGIVENESS, REPENTANCE, ETERNAL LIFE – and of course, first and most essential, THE NEW BIRTH. But many of us go through life without ever pausing really to look at these gifts, let alone unwrap them and make them our own. How casual and foolish we are!

The New Birth of Jesus Christ in the heart of a believer is a miracle just as striking as his first coming to Bethlehem; and like that it is silent, and mostly unnoticed by the world around. It is a miracle all the same, the first of many in the life of the believer. For the way in which a mortal human being can share the life of the eternal God is all miraculously wonderful from start to finish.

People who doubt the Virgin Birth of Christ usually also doubt the miracle of the New Birth of the believer. They are doing the foolish thing of denying something because it is as yet outside their experience – like Nicodemus. How sad to shut oneself off from the possibility of our loving God really intervening in our lives!

But he did intervene personally at Bethlehem, and so he will in your life – if only you bring yourself to give in to that wonderful love. He did not shirk danger and trouble when he came the first time, and he will not shirk the problems your life throws up, whatever they are. We do not deserve it, but *Where meek souls will receive Him, still the dear Christ enters in.*

When we enter into the New Birth for ourselves, all things start falling into place, the Virgin Birth among them. Mary's act of faith becomes the model for us all. We too can answer, 'I am the Lord's servant'; we too can take him at his word, and say, 'May it be to me as you have said'. It is the very first of miracles.

Monday – Lent 1

Nourishment for life

> Jesus said to them, 'I tell you the truth, unless you eat the flesh of the Son of Man and drink his blood, you have no life in you. Whoever eats my flesh and drinks my blood has eternal life, and I will raise him up at the last day. For my flesh is real food and my blood is real drink. Whoever eats my flesh and drinks my blood remains in me, and I in him. Just as the living Father sent me and I live because of the Father, so the one who feeds on me will live because of me. This is the bread that came down from heaven. Our forefathers ate manna and died, but he who feeds on this bread will live for ever.' JOHN 6:53–58

This is my body, said our Lord Jesus Christ at the Last Supper – words repeated by the Priest at every Eucharist. Christians down the centuries have agonised and argued over their meaning; but it is probably true that if their meaning could be precisely stated in words, then there would be no need for the Sacrament. As always with the Lord Jesus the most childlike approach is the best.

A symbol?
The 20th Century has a devastating way of analysing things and then writing them off. 'It's ONLY a symbol,' people say about the Sacrament, as if there were nothing else to it. On that basis this book is *only* a jumble of black marks on sheets of paper held together at their edges. Well yes, it is that. But it is not *only* that. For those black marks signify words, and the words are in sentences that convey ideas. By this book my mind may communicate with yours across barriers of space and time. No! The Sacrament is not just a symbol.

A keepsake?
Likewise the Sacrament is not just an object you keep to remind you of someone or something important to you. I have here a photograph of my friend. I keep it because it reminds me of things we shared and did together. Perhaps you have a gift or an ornament that reminds you of a loved one now gone; it is probably of no great value – except to you. Its value and meaning come from the life and experiences you shared together. To some extent the Sacrament serves that sort of

purpose; your 'remembrance' of Christ reminds you of his death for you on the Cross. It brings to mind what it cost him. It is a pledge of his love. It assures you that there will always be a place for you at his table. But that photograph cannot bring my friend any nearer. Your keepsake brings back only the memory of your loved one. It is a poor substitute for their actual presence. No! The Sacrament is not just a *keepsake*.

Nourishment?

I have said what the Sacrament is *not*; but let us be more positive and say what it *is*; and remember the right approach is the childlike one. The Sacrament is presented to us as *nourishment*; this is its form – bread and wine. Clearly it is not nourishment of a physical kind; it is intended to sustain us for eternal life. Our Lord Jesus Christ identified himself totally with that bread and wine. He means by it to nourish us with himself in the closest and most intimate union.

In a sense he intends all life to be a way of growing closer to him. Living, for the Christian is a sacramental experience – getting to know God through his creation and through those we share it with. But this is focused especially and uniquely in the Holy Communion. The Sacrament is a personal exchange between you and your Lord, and it enters into the deepest fabric of your lives – the real Lord Jesus touching the real you. If you find this hard, do not worry. Continue to receive the Sacrament, and ask the good Lord to make himself known to you in his own way. Above all do not agonise about understanding it. That does not matter. You can be nourished by wholesome food without knowing anything about proteins and vitamins and all that.

A photograph or a keepsake cannot bring back a loved one. But our Lord Jesus is victor over death, and he is here – here with me, and here with you; especially here with both us in the the bread and wine. It is a most personal exchange of love. It is as the squeeze of the hand between lovers; as the knowing glance between husband and wife; as the silence between those who have no need of words; as the happy smile between friends who are glad to meet. Such things are very nourishing, are they not? How much more so when the one who touches you is the eternal God!

Tuesday – Lent 1

A taste of salt

> You are the salt of the earth, but if the salt loses its saltiness, how can it be made salty again? It is no longer good for anything except to be thrown out and trampled by men.   MATTHEW 5:13

> John came neither eating nor drinking, and they say, 'He has a demon.' The Son of Man came eating and drinking, and they say, 'Here is a glutton and a drunkard, a friend of tax collectors and sinners.' But wisdom is proved right by her actions.   MATTHEW 11:18–19

You are the salt of the earth, said Jesus to his disciples. Salt is used to preserve foods – fish, bacon, and so on. It has the wonderful property of keeping decay at bay. And the true disciples of Jesus act as salt in the community. Jesus never told his followers they would be in a majority. But through prayer and example, and the living witness of the Christian fellowship, they were to wield an influence out of all proportion to their numbers. Salt is also used to enhance the flavour of food; potatoes, porridge, bread, are all tasteless if the salt is left out. In the same way, how dreary is the pattern of unrelieved worldliness when it takes over human affairs – just greed and self-seeking, and few of the things sought are really worth the struggle.

It is amazing that anyone ever followed Jesus, for he never promised them an easy life. Nowhere to lay your head, perhaps. He never looked for settled security, and never offered any to his followers. Hunger, danger, discomfort seemed to matter little to him when he was about his Father's business. But when good things were to hand nobody could enjoy them more whole-heartedly than our Jesus, particularly in good company – very dubious company, his enemies often thought. *A glutton and a drunkard*, they called him, as they watched his hilarious enjoyment of life. But it was all able to be left behind at the drop of a hat.

Only personal relationships were sacrosanct. Here he expected total loyalty, and his own commitment to his friends was unshakeable. That mixture of playful enjoyment with deep personal commitment to others, and always total obedience to his Father, is what Jesus calls saltiness. He intends his disciples to be salt in the community. He means the world to know through them the flavour of true human life, even when it does not recognise its source.

But if the salt loses its saltiness, how can it be made salty again? the Lord pointedly asks us. The rough salt of his day, dug from the shores of the Dead Sea, could indeed lose its saltiness. Leave it in a heap against the wall, and the rain would soon see to it that you had only a shrinking pile of tasteless grit.

In the life of our country much of the 'salt' has lost its saltiness, and we Christians are the ones responsible for this. Therefore decay, lack of purpose, and worldly standards, are taking over. Let the salt learn again to be *salty*. Let the disciples of Jesus once more learn their life-style from him. It could make all the difference.

Wednesday – Lent 1

Lessons in discipleship

When Jesus looked up and saw a great crowd coming towards him, he said to Philip, 'Where shall we buy bread for these people to eat?' Philip answered him, 'Eight months' wages would not buy enough bread for each one to have a bite!' Another of his disciples, Andrew, Simon Peter's brother, spoke up, 'Here is a boy with five small barley loaves and two small fish, but how far will they go among so many?'

Jesus said, 'Make the people sit down.' There was plenty of grass in that place, and the men sat down, about five thousand of them. Jesus then took the loaves, gave thanks, and distributed to those who were seated as much as they wanted. He did the same with the fish.

When they had all had enough to eat, he said to his disciples, 'Gather the pieces that are left over. Let nothing be wasted.' So they gathered them and filled twelve baskets with the pieces of the five barley loaves left over by those who had eaten.

After the people saw the miraculous sign that Jesus did, they began to say: 'Surely this is the Prophet who is to come into the world.' Jesus, knowing that they intended to come and make him king by force, withdrew again into the hills by himself.

When evening came, his disciples went down to the lake, where they got into a boat and set off across the lake for Capernaum. By now it was dark, and Jesus had not yet joined them. A strong wind was blowing and the waters grew rough. When they had rowed three or three and a half miles, they saw Jesus approaching the boat, walking on the water; and they were terrified. But he said to them, 'It is I; don't be afraid.' Then they were willing to take him into the boat, and immediately the boat reached the shore where they were heading.

JOHN 6:5–21

The story makes us look closely at our style of discipleship. What are our motives? When our hearts are laid bare, WHY do we follow Christ?

Following for fun
The crowd enjoyed it. It was exciting following Jesus. You might see a miracle. If you had any serious problem Jesus would help. And the

preaching was thrilling. It was fun, following Jesus. It stirred up such exciting dreams and hopes. Jesus could be USED to satisfy your needs, and to relieve the drab monotony of ordinary life. So the crowd wanted Jesus for their King — on their terms, of course. Here was someone to lead the revolt against the hated Romans, an ideal figurehead. There have always been crowds ready to follow Jesus like that.

Following in earnest

For the disciples it was rather different. Jesus took the initiative and posed them a practical problem — how to set up a picnic for 5000, miles from anywhere! But they had learnt one lesson: offer your miniscule efforts and resources to the Lord, and do it willingly. Then it is up to him. So the picnic started. Strangely it all seemed to work out. Nobody knew how. The disciples were not thinking about themselves. They were working too hard taking food to that crowd. But when it was all over, there was more than enough for them too — a whole basket of food each.

The Lord Jesus acted quickly to break up the party. A quick word — *into the boat and row to the other side* — and Jesus was gone up the hillside. They didn't see why, but they had to do it.

That was a tough night! Rowing into a strong headwind in the dark is not fun, even when Jesus says so.

Lesson: Much of the Christian life seems a hard and pointless slog, done for no other reason than obedience to Jesus. No doubt there were many muttered prayers in that boat: *Lord please make this wind die down — Lord I'm so cold and wet — Lord make the daylight come soon.* We've all done it, haven't we? But what the Lord did was to use the very adverse circumstances he had led them into. He walks in, triumphant over the wind and sea that troubled them.

Lesson: You need not ask the Lord to remove difficulties; rather, trust him to do great things right in the circumstances that afflict you. No sooner does Jesus come into the boat than they lift their eyes; and there, a few yards away, was the beach.

The crowd wanted Jesus as King — for their own ends. The disciples found that Jesus reigned even in the most awful situation. They arrived at their destination — and much sooner than they expected.

Thursday – Lent 1

Living water

Jacob's well was there, and Jesus, tired as he was from the journey, sat down by the well. It was about the sixth hour. When a Samaritan woman came to draw water, Jesus said to her, 'Will you give me a drink? ... The Samaritan woman said to him, 'You are a Jew and I am a Samaritan woman. How can you ask me for a drink?' ...

Jesus answered her, 'If you knew the gift of God and who it is that asks you for a drink, you would have asked him and he would have given you living water.... Everyone who drinks this water will be thirsty again, but whoever drinks the water I give him will never thirst. Indeed, the water I give him will become in him a spring of water welling up to eternal life.'

The woman said to him, 'Sir, give me this water.'   JOHN 4:6–15

On the last and greatest day of the Feast, Jesus stood and said in a loud voice, 'If a man is thirsty, let him come to me and drink. Whoever believes in me, as the Scripture has said, streams of living water will flow from within him.' By this he meant the Spirit, whom those who believed in him were later to receive. Up to that time the Spirit had not been given, since Jesus had not yet been glorified.   JOHN 7:37–39

Our Lord at his baptism received the power of the Holy Spirit to do his life's work. He did not attempt to start without that power. This same power he passes on to us. 'He will baptise you with the Holy Spirit and with fire,' John the Baptist had promised. (Luke 3:16) We too should not attempt to do God's work without the power of the Holy Spirit. This is given to us at our Baptism and confirmed at our Confirmation; but it needs to be released within us. The Lord Jesus had his own vivid way of putting this. He invited *thirsty* souls to *come to him* and *drink*. What does this imply?

1. We must want his power

Thirst can be one of the most compelling of human desires. Our Lord is saying that we must really *want* the power of the Holy Spirit. A casual desire will be satisfied with very little, and neither needs nor really wants his power; such a desire springs from little depth of commitment, and does not look to achieve much. The power of the Holy Spirit is for those who thirst.

2. We must come to Jesus
Our Lord Jesus Christ is the source of all blessings. Anything you seek from God is obtained through Jesus. You must come to *Jesus* for it. You may be wise to seek help from another Christian, perhaps your Parish Priest or some Christian Counsellor; and our Lord may well use them as channels of his grace. But *he* is the source of the blessing you seek, and it is important that you understand it.

3. We must drink
It would be perfectly possible to die of thirst with a limitless supply of fresh spring water before you – if you were foolish enough not to drink! You must not only believe in the power of God, you must also receive it in your life. Those who drink then find that the water becomes in them, as Jesus said, a spring of water welling up to eternal life for themselves and for others.

There is something very surprising about the places where springs of water choose to emerge from the ground. You would expect it to happen near the bottom of valleys. But often springs are to be found quite high up a hillside. No doubt there is a reason for this, if we could understand it. The 'springs' of the Holy Spirit are just as remarkable. It is amazing how God is able to reveal his love and power in the most unlikely people, and turn their lives into living springs of his life and joy.

The woman of Samaria was such a person. She was one for whom the streams of love had turned rank and foul. Yet Jesus saw in her a longing for real love, the love to be found only in the heart of God. You may have experienced only the very best of human love, but if you are to be the blessing God means you to be, you need that same life-giving touch.

Come yourself to the spring, the source of love and power, bubbling up from the heart of God in our Lord Jesus Christ. And you will find not only deep satisfaction, but also your own hard rock of a heart becoming under his hand a new spring welling up to eternal life. For God delights to do this miracle in the most unlikely people. *Sir, give me this water*, said the woman of Samaria, and was not disappointed.

Friday – Lent 1

A Spirit-led life

> Jesus, full of the Holy Spirit, returned from the Jordan and was led by the Spirit in the desert, where for forty days he was tempted by the devil. He ate nothing during those days, and at the end of them he was hungry. The devil said to him, 'If you are the Son of God, tell this stone to become bread.' Jesus answered, 'It is written: "Man does not live on bread alone."'
>
> The devil led him up to a high place and showed him in an instant all the kingdoms of the world. And he said to him, 'I will give you all their authority and splendour, for it has been given to me, and I can give it to anyone I want to. So if you worship me, it will all be yours.' Jesus answered, 'It is written: "Worship the Lord your God and serve him only."'
>
> The devil led him to Jerusalem and made him stand on the highest point of the temple. 'If you are the Son of God,' he said, 'throw yourself down from here. For it is written: "He will command his angels concerning you to guard you carefully; they will lift you up in their hands, so that you will not strike your foot against a stone."' Jesus answered, 'It says: "Do not put the Lord your God to the test."'
>
> LUKE 4:1–12

In the life of Jesus we see for the first time what it means to be filled with the Holy Spirit. God intends each of us to follow in the steps of Jesus and to walk on earth as he walked. Every believer may be filled with the Spirit; but in this, as in all things, we are committed to following the example of Jesus.

This story is a salutary reminder that the Spirit-led life is not going to be just thrills and excitement. These would follow in the life of Jesus, and much joy; but first of all in his temptations he works out for us all the implications of the Spirit-led life.

Flesh comes first

As Jesus sets out the Spirit first leads him into a period of heavy temptation; and the temptations start with the FLESH. He is tempted to meet a fleshly need (hunger) in an illicit way. Many Christians fresh from a rich spiritual experience are shocked to find themselves clobbered with fleshly temptations. God has seemed so real to them, Jesus so near, the Holy Spirit so in evidence – and then, greed, temper, lust, jealousy – and they hear Satan's whisper of despair: *Filled with the Spirit indeed! You must be joking.*

Many give up at this point, feeling it has all been an illusion. But through these difficult waters the Son of God charts a true path for us all. He has taken our flesh with all its desires and drives, and he will not deny or ignore any of them. He shows how human FLESH, with all its energies held in proper balance, may be filled out and completed by the Holy Spirit. That is the programme of the Incarnation – the Son of God taking human flesh and sanctifying it by his presence within it. So do not be surprised if the Holy Spirit starts his work by exposing and re-adjusting some matters of the flesh. It is definitely high on the agenda.

No compromise with evil

Satan offers Jesus the Kingdoms of the World without a struggle – a subtle move, for the Father had already promised that. Satan says he can have them now, with just a little compromise. But a little compromise leads to more; and such a path leads ever downwards until our lives are hopelessly tangled. Satan will always let us have what we want, if we accept his way of getting there.

But we know Satan's way – pretence, lies, wheeling and dealing, talking behind backs, strife and war – and Jesus will have none of it. God works through the quietness of faith and love. His way includes many Gethsemane's and Calvary's, and we must follow Jesus.

Avoid over-enthusiasm

The Lord Jesus is tempted to do a work so spectacular that people will be forced to believe. In the work of the Church we shall be tempted likewise. We *must* have results, and we must have them *now*. But Jesus is prepared to trust his Father to lay out his programme for him. His task is a simple obedience based on that trust. The Incarnation is all about being weak and letting God work powerfully.

That is it! You must trust your heavenly Father like that. Or do you feel you had better take things into your own hands? Satan's thrusts will find out every weak point of faith. The Lord Jesus refuses to hurry his Father's work. Timing and results he leaves in his good hands. That is what it means to be filled with the Spirit.

Saturday – Lent 1

The proof of faith

Jesus told them another parable: 'The kingdom of heaven is like a mustard seed, which a man took and planted in his field. Though it is the smallest of all your seeds, yet when it grows, it is the largest of the garden plants and becomes a tree, so that the birds of the air come and perch in its branches.'

He told them still another parable: 'The kingdom of heaven is like yeast that a woman took and mixed into a large amount of flour until it worked all through the dough.'   MATTHEW 13:31–33

I was being shown round the greenhouse where the gardener was at work. He was staring into the cupped palm of his hand; there seemed to be just a few crumbs of soil in it. 'Strange, isn't it?' he said. 'You wouldn't know there was a seed there in my hand; you'd never find it, however hard you looked. But it's there alright. I'll prove it to you.' He tipped the contents of his palm into the hollow prepared for it in a large flower pot. He patted the soil down and watered it from a can. 'Just give it a few weeks,' he said.

As we left the greenhouse it occurred to me what our Lord meant when he described the Kingdom of God, *like a mustard seed, which a man took and planted in his field* – and it grew and became a tree (it grows ten feet high in Palestine).

How hard it is to believe that the first vital contact of a human being with Jesus Christ can have such far-reaching effects. When someone first calls on the Lord for help and means it, this is like planting a small seed in the earth. There is almost nothing to show for it to start with. But under the good hand of God the seed grows until it fills all of life.

The same applies in parish life. When God's people start meeting to share in prayer, or gather at the Eucharist with a common intention, something momentous is begun. It does not seem so at first. But the yeast has started work in the dough, and the results under the good hand of God are incalculable and far-reaching.

Of course the seed needs watering, and there may be weeds that spring up in the soil beside it. But, look after it properly, and nothing can stop it developing into the plant God intended. So it is with someone who has turned to the Lord Jesus Christ.

Likewise the dough must be kept warm and in a place by itself. But treat it correctly, and soon you will see that it is full of the vigorous new life of the yeast. So it is with the church that prays and shares together.

Some weeks later I was ushered into that greenhouse. On the shelf was the same pot, but now in it grew a plant bearing a magnificent bloom. 'There's your proof,' said the gardener.

Take heart if you happen to be going through a dry patch in your Christian pilgrimage. The Church is full of people who can testify to the astonishing grace of our Lord Jesus Christ. He has not lost his skill, and you too will be sure of it before long.

Remember, O Lord, what you have wrought in us, and not what we deserve; and, as you have called us to your service, make us worthy of our calling; through Jesus Christ our Lord.

The Leonine Sacramentary
5th Century

Discussion Starters – *1st Week in Lent*

1. There are parallels between the New Birth of Christ in the heart of the believer and his conception in the womb of the Blessed Virgin Mary. In what ways should the attitude of a Christian echo the words of Mary at this point (page 18)?

2. What should it mean in your community to be *salty* (page 23)?

3. New commitment always seems to land disciples in new difficulties and temptations. This can be both bewildering and strengthening. How should we handle them?

2nd Week in Lent: Health for the Journey

FACING RESISTANCE IN OURSELVES

Teach us, good Lord, to serve you as you deserve; to give and not to count the cost; to fight and not to heed the wounds; to toil and not to seek for rest; to labour and not to ask for any reward, save that of knowing that we do your will; though Jesus Christ our Lord.

St Ignatius Loyola
16th Century

2nd Sunday in Lent

When Salvation comes

> Jesus entered Jericho and was passing through. A man was there by the name of Zacchaeus; he was a chief tax collector and was wealthy. He wanted to see who Jesus was, but being a short man he could not, because of the crowd. So he ran ahead and climbed a sycamore-fig tree to see him, since Jesus was coming that way.
>
> When Jesus reached the spot, he looked up and said to him, 'Zacchaeus, come down immediately. I must stay at your house today.' So he came down at once and welcomed him gladly.
>
> All the people saw this and began to mutter, 'He has gone to be the guest of a "sinner."' But Zacchaeus stood up and said to the Lord, 'Look, Lord! Here and now I give half of my possessions to the poor, and if I have cheated anybody out of anything, I will pay back four times the amount.'
>
> Jesus said to him, 'Today salvation has come to this house, because this man, too, is a son of Abraham. For the Son of Man came to seek and to save what was lost.'   LUKE 19:1–10

When Jesus walked into the house of Zacchaeus it caused a stir among the crowd. *The guest of a sinner*, they murmured in shocked voices. But Jesus said, '*SALVATION has come to this house.*' What did Jesus mean? What exactly had happened to Zacchaeus? What is SALVATION?

The word originally meant being whole or sound. It would be used of someone in the peak of physical condition. But it always referred to more than bodily health; it included a man's well-integrated personality, his sound and balanced relationships in family and community. Such a person had the wholeness that is *salvation*.

The word has always fitted easily into the Christian vocabulary. Being a Christian is a matter of restoring our vital relationship with God through Christ. This affects the rest of our lives – our other relationships are handled better, and our minds and bodies become healthier. We become sound and whole, as God meant us to be. We have received *salvation*. What a good word it is!

A restored relationship
Before we receive salvation we lack any real relationship with God.

This is set out in the ancient story of Adam and Eve, ever repeated in every human life, and always profoundly true. A point came when we deliberately rejected God's way and chose our own instead. The result is always the same. Like Adam and Eve, who hid themselves from God among the trees of the garden, we try and avoid him; and God for his part can have no fellowship with us while we cling to our phoney independence. In each of us sin has brought about its inevitable result, separation from God. Fortunately God loves us still, and has provided the way back in Christ. Jesus crossed the gulf that divided us from God; on the Cross he dealt with our sins, and now he is right alongside us by his Spirit, waiting to renew and rebuild our lost relationship with God and all that goes with it.

Salvation is Jesus

This is eternal life, he said, *that they may know you, the only true God, and Jesus Christ, whom you have sent.* (John 17:3) You cannot receive salvation *without* a new relationship with God, as you might buy a ticket for the cinema by applying at the box office. When you receive Jesus, salvation is not an incidental part of it; your new relationship with him *is* salvation. Salvation is not a by-product of some religious act, such as baptism or going forward at a Billy Graham meeting. Salvation is the new relationship with God which all Christian preaching is offering you.

Baptism opens the door to this, but you must enter. At every baptism Jesus is there beside the font; the Holy Spirit is there within the water; God himself says, 'This is my beloved child,' and offers an open welcome to that little unsuspecting baby. What an offer! And it is never withdrawn, even though that baby may and will show the usual human independence from God. At a later date he may come to his senses, and run to the arms of his Saviour and say, 'Why did they not tell me to do this before?'

If that child never turns to Christ, he becomes a walking contradiction – a Christian estranged from Christ, a child of God who doesn't belong, a baptised person not washed from his sins, someone booked for heaven but still separated from God. If this should be your condition, turn to Christ at once. He loves you and is right there beside you. Zacchaeus, at any rate, came down and welcomed Jesus into his house. Salvation had come, for Jesus had entered the door, and now Zacchaeus knew him – and would come to know him better and better through all eternity.

Monday – Lent 2

Full healing

When Jesus had called the Twelve together, he gave them power and authority to drive out all demons and to cure diseases, and he sent them out to preach the kingdom of God and to heal the sick. . . . So they set out and went from village to village, preaching the gospel and healing people everywhere.   LUKE 9:1–6

Is any of you in trouble? He should pray. Is anyone happy? Let him sing songs of praise. Is any one of you sick? He should call the elders of the church to pray over him and anoint him with oil in the name of the Lord. And the prayer offered in faith will make the sick person well; the Lord will raise him up. If he has sinned, he will be forgiven. Therefore confess your sins to each other and pray for each other so that you may be healed. The prayer of a righteous man is powerful and effective.   JAMES 5:13–16

When our Lord sent out the twelve disciples he gave them a twin commission: *Preach the gospel; heal the sick.* This is still the programme of the Christian Church. To some extent the healing ministry has been taken over by modern scientific medicine. You ring for the Doctor; and so you should – the Church is in no conflict with good medical practice (which the Church itself pioneered). But why not ring the Parish Priest also, and ask for the healing ministry of the Church. Most parishes now have some provision for a regular healing ministry; and many people make use of it, recognising that healing is an important part of the work of God in our lives. The letter of James gives clear instructions to the Church about this. Accordingly the Church prays, lays on hands, and anoints with oil, when it is appropriate to do so.

This ministry probably disappeared from general use in the Middle Ages because of misguided assumptions about miracles and saints. They thought that miracles were a proof of saintliness. Saintliness in the Minister must always help, for it implies a close walk with the Lord. But miracles of healing do not depend on us but on the Lord; they are an undeserved gift of his grace. If you are going to wait for your Parish Priest to show signs of great sanctity before you ask for the ministry of healing, you may have to wait a long time!

Are people healed? That is the question in your mind. Those who have practised the healing ministry for years have no doubt about it. *Of course* Jesus heals! It is my personal conviction that the Lord *always* heals. Not sometimes, but ALWAYS, though often his healing touch is known in ways we had not looked for: the sick person dies, but receives inner healing; or healing spreads out into the family situation and the community. We must remember that our Lord is in the business of healing a whole world – and so he will in the fullness of time. Very rarely does he give us anything that amounts to a *proof*. He prefers the healing ministry to be unobtrusive, gentle, and loving, letting faith produce its own sort of inner proof. *See that you tell no one*, was usually his command to someone he had healed.

Many people fail to see full healing because they ask the Lord to heal their symptoms, when he would address the root cause of their trouble. Why pray about a headache, when the real problem is compulsive over-work or unforgiven sin? Why pray about an ulcer, while gnawing anxiety consumes the life God gave you? Why seek healing for arthritis, if hidden (and perhaps forgotten) bitterness has poisoned your system for years and is being held back from the loving touch of Jesus?

Much of our sickness arises in a miserable tangle of false habits and spoilt personal relationships; and these in turn have their origins in the sicknesses of others. Jesus loves you too much to give a superficial physical healing that might leave you still a wounded and battered personality. He wants to give you complete wholeness of body, mind and spirit. Some of his work in your life will not be finished this side of eternity; but much of it will, if you allow him. We are all inherently blind about ourselves; so this is an area where you need to involve someone else to help you. Have a word with your Parish Priest, and pray with him for healing – *full* healing.

Tuesday – Lent 2

Help with confession

> Jesus got up from the meal, took off his outer clothing, and wrapped a towel round his waist. After that, he poured water into a basin and began to wash his disciples' feet, drying them with the towel that was wrapped around him.
>
> He came to Simon Peter, who said to him, 'Lord, are you going to wash my feet?' Jesus replied, 'You do not realise now what I am doing, but later you will understand.' 'No,' said Peter, 'you shall never wash my feet.' Jesus answered, 'Unless I wash you, you have no part with me.' 'Then, Lord,' Simon Peter replied, 'not just my feet but my hands and my head as well!'
>
> Jesus answered, 'A person who has had a bath needs only to wash his feet; his whole body is clean. And you are clean, though not every one of you.' For he knew who was going to betray him, and that was why he said not every one was clean. . . . 'Do you understand what I have done for you?' he asked them. 'You call me "Teacher" and "Lord," and rightly so, for that is what I am. Now that I, your Lord and Teacher, have washed your feet, you also should wash one another's feet. I have set you an example that you should do as I have done for you.'
>
> JOHN 13:4–15

This passage teaches the need for cleansing from sin before we share in the Lord's Supper. It also teaches us not to think of any tasks we do for others as too menial. But the real concern of our Lord was with the sin that clung to their lives. The dust from the streets was of no consequence; the tensions between them mattered enormously. Sin must be washed away before the Supper could start. I cannot exaggerate the importance of examining our lives regularly. It is a weekly job, and not to be shirked before we come to the Holy Communion. *A man ought to examine himself before he eats of the bread and drinks of the cup.* (1 Corinthians 11:28)

Indeed why wait for Saturday if there is something on your conscience? Confess it at once, wherever you are, at home or out shopping. Things between you and God need never be clouded at all. But you should also make time for regular self-examination. Your conscience is a blunt instrument, which easily fails to notice some glaring fault. So let your mind run back over the week; the Holy Spirit will prompt you if something needs to be confessed. *If we confess our sins, he is faithful and just and will forgive us our sins and purify us from all unrighteousness.* (1 John 1:9)

A baptised person who has turned to Christ is fundamentally clean – only the dirt from the week's journey through life needs to be washed away. *A person who has had a bath needs only to wash his feet.* Judas Iscariot was there too, but his heart was far from the Lord; no foot-washing was going to help him unless he gave up his sin and turned to the Lord for a fundamental cleansing.

The help of a priest

You, on your own, have complete access to God through Christ; you can reach out to him without the help of anyone else. But the New Testament regards the Ministry of Reconciliation as a normal part of Church life. *You also should wash one another's feet,* says our Lord. You do not need the ministry of a priest to be forgiven. But you may be wise to involve him. Here are some good reasons:

(a) We are all blind about our own faults; a word from the priest may help you see the real source of some sin that troubles you. We all need counselling from time to time, even if we do not make a formal confession. Have a word with your parish priest about it – or call on any other priest; Church rules have always allowed this.

(b) There are circumstances which make forgiveness hard to believe in: loss and bereavement, for instance, or some sorts of sickness. The ministry of a priest can then be a great help. Forgiveness and healing are linked, as yesterday's passage emphasised: *Confess your sins to each other . . . so that you may be healed.*

(c) Many Christians have found that a regular practice of formal confession is for them a strong protection against temptation. The thought of having to put that sin into words is a real deterrent!

The first time is the hardest. If you *ought* to do it (and only *you* can decide that), make an appointment and get on with it! Make a list of your sins and use it during the confession; otherwise your memory will let you down! Your confession must be as full as you can make it; but what you cannot remember the Lord passes over. You are not confessing to the priest but to the Lord; he is the one who washes your feet, using the words of the priest to do it. The sin is then forgiven and forgotten: *I will forgive their wickedness and will remember their sins no more.* (Jeremiah 31:34)

Wednesday – Lent 2

Complete conversion

Meanwhile, Saul was still breathing out murderous threats against the Lord's disciples. He went to the high priest and asked him for letters to the synagogues in Damascus, so that if he found any there who belonged to the Way, whether men or women, he might take them as prisoners to Jerusalem. As he neared Damascus on his journey, suddenly a light from heaven flashed around him. He fell to the ground and heard a voice say to him, 'Saul, Saul, why do you persecute me?' 'Who are you, Lord?' Saul asked.

'I am Jesus, whom you are persecuting,' he replied. 'Now get up and go into the city, and you will be told what you must do.' . . . So they led him by the hand into Damascus. For three days he was blind, and did not eat or drink anything.

In Damascus there was a disciple named Ananias. The Lord called to him in a vision, . . . 'Go to the house of Judas on Straight Street and ask for a man from Tarsus named Saul, for he is praying. In a vision he has seen a man named Ananias come and place his hands on him to restore his sight.'

'Lord,' Ananias answered, 'I have heard many reports about this man. . . . And he has come here with authority from the chief priests to arrest all who call on your name.'

But the Lord said to Ananias, 'Go! This man is my chosen instrument to carry my name before the Gentiles and their kings and before the people of Israel.' . . .

Then Ananias went to the house and entered it. Placing his hands on Saul, he said, 'Brother Saul, the Lord – Jesus, who appeared to you on the road as you were coming here – has sent me so that you may see again and be filled with the Holy Spirit.' Immediately, something like scales fell from Saul's eyes, and he could see again. He got up and was baptised, and after taking some food, he regained his strength.   ACTS 9:1–19

The Church we have inherited owes its form and its doctrine under the hand of God very much to one man, Saul of Tarsus, later to be called St Paul. His later achievement flowed from the thoroughness of his conversion, and this depended on three acts of obedience. You do well to ponder these, for many Christians remain ineffective because they lack a *complete* conversion.

Obedience to the light he had

Saul was on the road that day simply because he was convinced God wanted him to oppose the new Christian way that was growing among his people. It was an act of obedience to what he thought was the will of God – mistakenly, as it happens. There is no other attitude with which to embark on a spiritual pilgrimage. Whether you prove to be right or wrong, do what you believe God wants – though persecution of our opponents can never be the Christian option.

Obedience to others Gods sends

When Saul had realised that the one from whom the light came was Jesus, the carpenter of Nazareth, he is told, *Go into the city, and you will be TOLD what you must do*. The person God sends is an unknown disciple in the Church at Damascus called Ananias. So Saul, the brilliant young Rabbi, has to accept instruction and teaching from a nobody for the Lord's sake. Much of the teaching would be quite contrary to the habits of thought of a learned Rabbi. But humbly he accepts it and DOES what he is told. There is no other attitude with which to move forward from our conversion.

Obedience to the Spirit of Grace

Much of the teaching about grace that Saul was later to pass on to us must have been learnt from that humble disciple who came to him in his blindness. How scared poor Ananias must have been! Prison and death might well await him. The man he was to greet in the Lord's name was none other than the arch-persecutor from Jerusalem.

But he knew he must extend the welcome of grace to ANYONE the Lord put him in touch with. *BROTHER Saul*, he addresses him, with his arms and heart wide open. His act of love might have been repulsed, but it made no difference. The only attitude for a true follower of Jesus is the same open-hearted acceptance of everyone – just like Jesus himself. GRACE, it is called. The Lord requires it of all who follow him. It became Saul's way, praise the Lord. Make sure it is yours also.

Thursday – Lent 2

Whose body is it?

> But God has combined the members of the body and has given greater honour to the parts that lacked it, so that there should be no division in the body, but that its parts should have equal concern for each other. If one part suffers, every part suffers with it; if one part is honoured, every part rejoices with it. Now you are the body of Christ, and each one of you is a part of it.   1 CORINTHIANS 12:24–27

> Speaking the truth in love, we will in all things grow up into him, who is the Head, that is, Christ. From him the whole body, joined and held together by every supporting ligament, grows and builds itself up in love, as each part does its work.   EPHESIANS 4:15–16

When Saul of Tarsus met the risen Christ on the Damascus road, the Lord said: *I am Jesus, whom you are persecuting.* How could it be that Saul, a man on earth, was persecuting Jesus, the Lord in Heaven? It was only the followers of Jesus that Saul had been flogging, stoning, and putting in prison.

Saul realised then, in the moment of his conversion, that those who belonged to Jesus were truly the limbs of his body. If I cut my finger, I am the only person who feels the pain. You may wince in sympathy; you may imagine how unpleasant it must be; but you cannot actually feel the pain. Yet injuries and troubles experienced by those who belong to the Lord are all truly felt in his heart. His is no mere sympathy, but a true sharing of our sorrow – and our joy. There is a 'nerve' that joins your heart and his. St Paul described Jesus Christ as *the head of the body*, in whom all 'nerves' end, and from whom come the direction and co-ordination that heal and bring new life to the world. To look at the Church as the Body of Christ can guide the way we approach a time of taking stock such as Lent.

Each belongs to all

As an individual member of the Body you need to attend to your own relationship with the Lord and seek to develop it, using the means of grace he has given you – prayer, Bible reading, Eucharist, confession, worship. But this is no mere personal pursuit of holiness. For in the

Body other members depend on your relationship with the Lord. *From him the whole Body, joined and held together by every supporting ligament, grows and builds itself up in love, as each part does its work.* If your Christian life is at a low level, the whole Body suffers, and others who might be blessed through you do not receive support from your presence. The quality of your life and of your relationships within the Body play an important part in the outreach of the Church.

All belong to each

That, however, is not the whole story. The fellowship and support you share together in your local Church are very important, but your Parish is only a small part of the whole Body. You could think of yourselves as neighbouring fingers on a hand, say; but that hand is useless without the rest of the body. We depend on, and have a part to play in, the life of the whole world-wide Church.

We in England are a very comfortable part of the Body, well-wrapped against persecution and deprivation. Other parts of Christ's Body live in harshly exposed environments. There can be no health in the Church as long as we remain unconcerned and uninvolved in their struggles. *I tell you the truth. Whatever you did for one of the least of these brothers of mine, you did for me.* (Matthew 25:40) Nor can the Body of Christ do its work in the world if some parts of it are sick. *If one part suffers, every part suffers with it.* Besides it is *Christ's* Body, and he feels its sickness himself. Lent is a time to re-think and re-adjust our relationships within the Church   locally and world wide.

Friday – Lent 2

Dealing with doubt

> Then Job replied: If only I knew where to find him; if only I could go to his dwelling! I would state my case before him and fill my mouth with arguments. I would find out what he would answer me, and consider what he would say. . . . But he stands alone, and who can oppose him? He does whatever he pleases.   JOB 23:3–13

> Will the Lord reject us for ever? Will he never show his favour again? Has his unfailing love vanished for ever? Has his promise failed for all time? Has God forgotten to be merciful? . . . Your ways, O God, are holy. What God is so great as our God?   PSALM 77:7–13

For many years now I have had not the slightest doubt about any doctrine in the Creeds. But above all, I believe in and trust the God that the Creeds, the Bible and the Church talk about. Actually that is the difficult part. God's ways are so strange – as poor Job found. He makes us trust him precisely when we cannot understand. How should we deal with doubts and questionings in our minds? I was not always so confident about the Church's teaching, and I want to share with you the way I discovered out of the fog of doubtings. There are three different kinds of doubt, but only one of them is fatal. Let us deal with the non-fatal ones first.

Not understanding God's way
This sort of doubt is quite normal, indeed inevitable. Even Jesus experienced it. *'My God, my God, why have you forsaken me?'* he cries from the cross. (Matthew 26:46) He did not understand what his Father was doing at that awful moment. But notice that even then it was *MY God*; his relationship with his Father remained rock-like and unquestioned. *My thoughts are not your thoughts, neither are your ways my ways, declares the Lord.* (Isaiah 55:8) Mortal Man dealing with infinite God is bound to find this difficulty.

Doubting Christian doctrines
This is more serious; for you will never be a strong Christian if important doctrines fail to take proper root in your life. This was my

initial experience. I doubted most of the Creed, had no use for the Church, and saw little point in the Bible. But I had placed my faith in the Lord Jesus Christ; and it seemed a sort of disloyalty to him to treat these things so.

Then the thought occurred to me, 'I do not understand this, but Jesus does. Why not ask him?' So there began a period in my life in which one by one I laid the problems before the Lord. It was never very long before the answer came. I would hear or read something, and understand. Sometimes I saw that I did not need to know the answer to that – not yet. In general simple obedience brought understanding. It was not long before I knew that the Bible was the Word of God, for he had spoken to me through it; and I knew that the Church was the Body of Christ, for he had blessed me through its ministers and fellowship. I commend this way out of doubt to you.

Doubting God's goodness

This is the third kind of doubt, and it is fatal; for it kills our relationship with God. It happens when we doubt God's goodness, or question his love for us. This was the primal temptation in the Garden of Eden. *Did God really say that?* questions the serpent (Genesis 3:1), and sows the seed of doubt. Had God an ulterior motive? Was that command good, or was it just an arbitrary rule? Was it true they would die if they ate the forbidden fruit? The goodness, love, and truthfulness of God were all called into question in that first hissing whisper from the Enemy of souls.

How do you deal with the onset of this kind of doubt? Lay it before God immediately. Throw back the door of your heavenly Father's chamber, and cast it in his face – with real indignation, if that is how you feel. Much of the Psalms are this sort of prayer. *Will the Lord reject us for ever? . . . Has his unfailing love vanished? . . .* Then there is a pause as God responds quietly to the bitter complaint of his child, and the tune changes – *Your ways, O God, are holy. What God is so great as our God?*

Much depends on being often with the Lord's people. Doubt has little chance of hurting us when we are with others who know his goodness. Doubt must never be met with condemnation and rejection. Many strong Christians have known times of severe doubt. So do not be worried by it; the good Lord knows how to help you through it. But watch out for that third kind, won't you? For it is fatal.

Saturday – Lent 2

The Good Master

> Do not merely listen to the word, and so deceive yourselves. Do what it says. Anyone who listens to the word but does not do what it says is like a man who looks at his face in a mirror and, after looking at himself, goes away and immediately forgets what he looks like. But the man who looks intently into the perfect law that gives freedom, and continues to do this, not forgetting what he has heard, but doing it – he will be blessed in what he does.
>
> If anyone considers himself religious and yet does not keep a tight rein on his tongue, he deceives himself and his religion is worthless. Religion that God our Father accepts as pure and faultless is this: to look after orphans and widows in their distress and to keep oneself from being polluted by the world.   JAMES 1:22–27

We human beings find it very difficult to accept rules of conduct given by someone else, even by God. It irks us that anyone should dictate to us; it seems to limit our freedom. But take a lesson from your dog. What does he do when you take his lead from its hook? He goes wild with excitement! Yet it would be hard to think of anything more freedom-limiting and imposed-by-authority than a dog's lead. It is the very symbol of obedience and submission.

But that is not how your dog sees it. For him it is the thing that makes possible a walk with Master, and expresses Master's concern for his safety. O the glorious freedom of such a walk! – trotting obediently at his side. What could be more exciting!

It is a pity we do not see God's rules and guidelines the same way. There are many situations when your dog can be let off the lead; much of the time a well-trained dog can dispense with the lead altogether. He knows what is expected of him, and can be trusted to behave himself. In the same way there is much of life when God is happy to let us follow our own noses without restriction.

But when the traffic is heavy, and unsuspected dangers lurk round the corner, the lead has to be used. And there are times when our Master bids us accept his restraining hand (his *yoke*, he called it – Matthew 11:28–30); otherwise in our foolishness we may be driven from his side and lost.

46

He is the Good Master, and what matters more than anything else is being with him, walking in the glorious freedom of his abundant life and love. St John was sure of it: *This is love for God: to obey his commands. And his commands are not burdensome* (1 John 5:3). *Oh, how I love your law!* cried the Psalmist (Psalm 119:97). Yes, God wants us to revel in it. The yoke of Jesus is never burdensome, but rather the means of sharing the glorious freedom of belonging deeply to him.

Visit, Lord we pray, our homes, and drive from them all the snares of the evil one; let your holy angels dwell in them to preserve all who live there in peace; and may your blessing be upon us evermore; through Jesus Christ our Lord.

From the Order of Compline

Discussion Starters – *2nd Week in Lent*

1. We can all see how desirable it is to have wholeness of body, mind and spirit. Do you think it is hard to receive wholeness?

2. The first words of Jesus to the paralytic man let down through the roof were: *Your sins are forgiven* (Mark 2:5). Trace the part confession and forgiveness of sin play in making us whole.

3. Look critically at the pattern of relationships within your church fellowship and with other Christians. How should these relationships protect your faith and strengthen it?

3rd Week in Lent: Progress through Prayer

SHARING THE TASK WITH GOD

Almighty God, you know our necessities before we ask, and our ignorance in asking: set free your servants from all anxious thoughts for the morrow; give us contentment with your good gifts; and confirm our faith that according as we seek your kingdom, you will not suffer us to lack any good thing; through Jesus Christ our Lord.

St Augustine of Hippo
5th Century

3rd Sunday in Lent

Through Christ our Lord

I tell you the truth, anyone who has faith in me will do what I have been doing. He will do even greater things than these, because I am going to the Father. And I will do whatever you ask in my name, so that the Son may bring glory to the Father. You may ask me for anything in my name, and I will do it.

If you love me, you will obey what I command. I will ask the Father, and he will give you another Counsellor to be with you for ever – the Spirit of truth. The world cannot accept him, because it neither sees him nor knows him. But you know him, for he lives with you and will be in you.   JOHN 14:12–17

In that day you will no longer ask me anything. I tell you the truth, my Father will give you whatever you ask in my name. Until now you have not asked for anything in my name. Ask and you will receive, and your joy will be complete.   JOHN 16:23–24

The promises of Jesus on prayer are quite staggering. There seems no limit to what we might do – with just one qualification: it must be prayer *in his name*. What do we mean by PRAYER IN THE NAME OF JESUS? Let us try and unwrap that vital phrase a bit, since many people lack joy and much else in the Christian life because they have not prayed in the name of Jesus.

As his representative

As we pray we must be his representatives, as though it was Jesus himself praying; we need to be thinking about things his way, with his priorities. The difficulty is that our way of looking at things is often so very different from his. How are we to pray in the name of Jesus when our thoughts are running on a different track to his? It is a real problem. Our inherent selfishness and smallness of mind stop us from lifting our eyes and seeing things in the same way as Jesus. We need to change the points over so that our prayers run on his track.

Our Lord sees the problem, and so he promises to ask the Father to give us *another Counsellor, the Spirit of truth*. He refers to the Holy Spirit as *another* Counsellor, for while Jesus had been with them he had been their Counsellor. When they asked him, *Lord teach us to pray* (Luke 11:1), he did; and they learnt to absorb his attitudes. Now he was leaving, and they needed *another Counsellor*. The only way to move our prayers off the closed and sterile circuit of our own minds is with the help of the Holy Spirit. We need to admit that we need this help, and that it is readily given: *The Spirit helps us in our weakness. We do not know what we ought to pray, but the Spirit himself intercedes for us.* (Romans 8:26)

'Does it work?'

I often meet sad Christians, who have tried really hard with prayer, but the effort has eventually collapsed within them. 'Does it work?' they ask with unhappy realism. Does IT work indeed! Why do they say IT? While we think like that there is no chance at all that IT will work. Prayer is not a magic procedure by which we twist the arm of an impersonal universe to oblige us in our daily lives. Rather we should ask, 'Does HE work?' which is the same as asking 'Is God real?' And then, is he interested in the small concerns of my daily life? Or to put it another way, 'Does God love me?' Here is the real issue. Do you want a God who will intervene lovingly in your life? If you do not, then there is no other God; there is no IT to which you can appeal. You are on your own.

God makes it possible

But now I hope you are asking another question: 'How can I have dealings with this God?' The answer is simple; it is too important to be allowed to be complicated. GOD HIMSELF HAS MADE IT POSSIBLE FOR YOU. He sent his Son Jesus into this world to come right alongside us and bridge the gap between God and Man, since Jesus was (and is) both God and Man.

Now he offers through Jesus the opportunity to enter into a real fellowship with him. That is prayer. If we ask for it, he will give us through his Spirit that fellowship in Jesus. He will intervene in our lives in perfect love; and in unity of heart and mind we will seek and desire what he wants. That is prayer in the name of Jesus.

Monday – Lent 3

Asking for things

> Ask and it will be given to you; seek and you will find; knock and the door will be opened to you. For everyone who asks receives; he who seeks finds; and to him who knocks, the door will be opened.
>
> Which of you, if his son asks for bread, will give him a stone? Or if he asks for a fish, will give him a snake? If you, then, though you are evil, know how to give good gifts to your children, how much more will your Father in heaven give good gifts to those who ask him!
>
> MATTHEW 7:7–11

Jesus said: 'Ask and it will be given to you.' Nothing could be more definite. 'But,' you say, 'I *have* asked for things, and not been given them. I am disillusioned.' And you grumble that the Lord does not seem to keep his promise. I suggest that you may not have looked closely enough at his words. He seems to repeat the promise three times, using different forms of words. But our Lord never said things merely for their verbal effect. There is a sequence in this simple teaching, and we need to look at it. ASK – SEEK – KNOCK. That is the sequence our Lord will lead us in as we pray.

1. Ask

He invites us to ask God for things in the simplest possible way, as a child would ask his parent for something. You do not need to be introspective and wonder whether your motives are right, or whether you are being selfish. You need it, or someone else does – or just you want it, and it seems *good*. So you ask. There are three possible answers to such prayers, as there are three colours in a traffic light: *green* – yes, by all means; *red* – no, definitely not, think again; or *amber* – wait, not yet. It is the amber light that tries our patience. It forces us to stop and query what exactly we are asking for. The blessing that seemed clear enough when we first expressed it, suddenly looks blurred, and we see all sorts of branching possibilities within it.

2. Seek

What should you be asking for? What is it you really mean by this urgent unformed desire that you cannot quite put into words? So you enter on a time of searching – searching for the thing God wants to give you, the thing you most want, if you could identify it. This searching is not a lonely task, however. It is all part of that strange interplay of your mind and the mind of Jesus, which is what prayer is all about. You become gradually aware of the way he sees things; you begin to sense the objectives in his mind. It is a long process sometimes, requiring much perseverance, and capable of causing much discomfort and inner turmoil.

3. Knock

Sometimes I call at a house, and I know there is some elderly person there who wants to see me. I go up to the front door and knock and knock. No answer, and I wonder if something is wrong. Then I notice a card with faded writing pinned near the knocker – *Please use side door*. So I do just that, and am greeted at once. I was knocking on the wrong door, and until that message had sunk in I could get no further. We need to seek and seek until we find the right door.

With what joyous certainty we finally 'knock' in the total confidence that this is the right door. Sometimes that elderly person has seen me coming, and opens the door even as I raise my hand to knock. It is the same with our God. As you 'knock' the good Lord is right there, and you know that the real answer to your prayer is God himself. You came asking for *things*; but he gives us *himself*. Indeed the things are only the means by which he gives himself. It is a sort of miracle he loves to work.

Tuesday – Lent 3

The love that constrains

> Paul and his companions travelled throughout the region of Phrygia and Galatia, having been kept by the Holy Spirit from preaching the word in the province of Asia. When they came to the border of Mysia, they tried to enter Bithynia, but the Spirit of Jesus would not allow them to. So they passed by Mysia and went down to Troas. During the night Paul had a vision of a man of Macedonia standing and begging him. 'Come over to Macedonia and help us.' After Paul had seen the vision, we got ready at once to leave for Macedonia, concluding that God had called us to preach the gospel to them.
>
> From Troas we put out to sea and sailed straight for Samothrace, and the next day on to Neapolis. From there we travelled to Philippi, a Roman colony and the leading city of that district of Macedonia. And we stayed there several days.   ACTS 16:6–12

Nothing cements our relationship with the Lord more truly than accepting his guidance on life's path, and then letting him get us there in his own way. *Show me your ways, O Lord, teach me your paths*, cries the Psalmist (Psalm 25:3). This needs to be the sincere prayer of our hearts; we let him choose both our destination and the path to be followed; and then the hand of the Lord upon us becomes real in a way it has not been before.

The Acts of the Apostles is full of stories of God guiding those early Christians in their work. One of the most striking examples of this was the way St Paul and his companions were directed to take the gospel into Europe instead of Asia Minor.

I would love to know how the Spirit kept them from preaching in Asia. Did they all have sore throats? And what did the Spirit do to prevent them going into Bithynia? Were there landslides on the road? Or were they turned back at some frontier? Or was it just that they felt no peace in their hearts as they took the wrong turning. We don't know. But guided they were, and saw the hand of the Lord in it all. Here are some principles this story teaches us.

Make a start anyway
St Paul starts on the missionary journey, even though he does not

know where he is going. It is no use sitting at home saying, 'If God wants me to be a missionary, he will make it clear to me.' He *does* want you to be a missionary, or at least share in the missionary task of the whole Church, at home if not abroad. So set out on the journey. Nobody can steer a stationary boat; get it moving in the water, and then a touch on the tiller will swing it round the right way. God guides us when we set out, and not before.

Frustrations and open doors

St Paul is not put off by frustrations; he sees these as the means God is using to guide him. I expect there were many temptations to think he had got it wrong, and had better go home. Prevented from turning left into Asia or right into Bithynia he just carried straight on until he got to the sea, and then there was no further to go! At least the Lord's mysterious method has made Paul pliable in his hand; he is ready for anything now, and agog to see what the Lord is going to do next. He was now ripe for that little breath of guidance that pointed him across the sea to Macedonia and Europe. And then everything fitted together to confirm it – a ship ready, a fair wind, and a quick journey to their destination.

A deepening relationship

St Paul seems to experience the Lord in an increasingly personal way as the story unfolds. First it is the *Holy Spirit* who hedges in his path; then it is the *Spirit of Jesus*. It means the same thing, you say. But I think it also conveys the thought that, when the landslide blocked the road, or whatever it was, the Lord Jesus seemed to be right there, and he knew it was alright.

It is a most relaxing thing to know the guiding hand of the Lord. For with a God who loves us like that it is certainly all going to be well, come what may. We may not achieve *our* objectives; but he will achieve *his*, and that is what matters. And the path he takes will be one of growing fellowship with him.

> *Good and upright is the Lord;*
> *therefore he instructs sinners in his ways.*
> *He guides the humble in what is right*
> *and teaches them his way.*
> *All the ways of the Lord are loving and faithful*
> *for those who keep the demands of his covenant.* Psalm 25:8–10

Wednesday – Lent 3

Bringing it to Christ

> For I received from the Lord what I also passed on to you: The Lord
> Jesus, on the night he was betrayed, took bread, and when he had given
> thanks, he broke it and said, 'This is my body, which is for you; do this
> in remembrance of me.' In the same way, after supper he took the cup,
> saying, 'This is the new covenant in my blood; do this, whenever you
> drink it, in remembrance of me.' For whenever you eat this bread and
> drink this cup, you proclaim the Lord's death until he comes.
>
> 1 CORINTHIANS 11:23–26

It is significant that the substances our Lord took to form the Sacrament of Holy Communion were bread and wine. We do not bring to the Lord's table just his gifts, wheat and grapes, but what our labour has made them into, bread and wine. The Sacrament of Baptism is different. There we use water, elemental and just as God gave it.

But in the Sacrament by which we are nourished and sustained in the Christian life our Lord wants us to bring to his Table things that represent our life and work. We come offering him not just the life he has given us, but what we have made of our lives. We are to come with our successes and failures, with our joys and woes, with our hurts and wounds and blemishes. This is how he wants us to come, just as we are. And this is how he receives us, just as we are. Sins confessed find forgiveness; mistakes admitted incur no reproach; a life felt as worthless is given its only true value, namely that the Son of God counts you worth dying for.

Just as we are

This is the only way to come, as every priest has had to learn. For there have been times when he must celebrate the Eucharist at the appointed hour; but for reasons which may or may not be his fault something is seriously amiss – perhaps disaster has struck, or some personal relationship is in difficulties. Emotions are strained, nerves are on edge, and he wishes he could be alone for a few hours to get over it. If feelings were any guide (and they never are at such a point), he would keep away from the Lord's Table that day. But he may not do that; the Lord's people are waiting.

So with leaden heart he goes through the motions. And as he takes the bread and the wine and places them on the Altar, he knows that he is bringing before the Lord his life and the lives of any others involved; and he knows yet again that the Lord is receiving them into his hands, gently, lovingly, just as they are, and is drawing the whole trouble into his perfect sacrifice on the cross.

His renewing presence

What the priest does at the Altar is not only for himself but on behalf of the whole congregation. So if you are distraught, do not stay away; come, as you are, and lay it all silently before the Lord when the bread and the wine are brought to the Table. The Lord will accept your distress and trouble quietly, thanking his Father that you have brought it to him, for he alone can handle it. Then he breaks it – and it will have no further power to damage your life. Finally, in the bread and wine, he gives our lives back to us, full of his renewing presence and love.

Fortunately things are not always as bad as this when we attend the Holy Communion! We come usually with no more in the way of anxieties and pressures than the next person. Life may well be on an even keel, and we feel we are coping. But the principle is the same. We come, just as we are, offering ourselves and all that we are to him. He receives us lovingly, gives thanks, and breaks – yes, even our best moments must be brought to the cross – and in his own special way nourishes us with his presence.

The one perfect sacrifice

The only true offering that Mankind may present before the Father is that of his Son upon the cross, made once for us all. At the Eucharist the priest offers to God that *full, perfect, and sufficient sacrifice and oblation*, made once long ago. Nothing we could do, and nothing we might offer, could add anything to that. It is already perfect and complete. But graciously God allows our lives to be drawn into that offering, to share in the blessings Christ won for us there. It cost him everything. To us it is a free gift, to be received *by faith with thanksgiving*.

There is a place for you at his Table, guaranteed for you by the Son of God himself. So do not stay away, whatever befalls you. Come, just as you are, not pretending to be anything special at all – just grateful to belong.

Thursday – Lent 3

A fruiting vine

I am the true vine and my Father is the gardener. He cuts off every branch in me that bears no fruit, while every branch that does bear fruit he trims clean so that it will be even more fruitful. You are already clean because of the word I have spoken to you. Remain in me, and I will remain in you. No branch can bear fruit by itself; it must remain in the vine. Neither can you bear fruit unless you remain in me.

I am the vine; you are the branches. If a man remains in me and I in him, he will bear fruit; apart from me you can do nothing. If anyone does not remain in me, he is like a branch that is thrown away and withers; such branches are picked up, thrown into the fire and burned. If you remain in me and my words remain in you, ask whatever you wish, and it will be given you. This is to my Father's glory, that you bear much fruit, showing yourselves to be my disciples.   JOHN 15:1–8

The Holy Spirit is given to make the Church fruitful. Fruit is for reproduction. We are apt to forget this. Sometimes we talk as though the fruit of the Spirit was only a matter of godly living and outgoing love. Certainly fruit must be sweet to the taste. In nature its sweetness is what attracts the birds and animals (and Man) to take it. But the biological purpose is to spread the seed widely. Yes, the Church must be Christ-like; but the purpose is to spread the knowledge of Christ to the ends of the world.

The fruitless branch

Some branches have much show of leaves, and look really good. But closer inspection reveals an absence of fruit – no grapes! What is to be done? There is nothing for it but to cut the branch away; it is taking up space needed for a useful branch.

Some churches have nice services, the buildings are well kept, the finances are in order, and everything looks fine. But there is no fruit. People are not being drawn to know Christ and to make him known. We human beings never see the whole picture, and must not be too critical; but the heavenly gardener does. In his wisdom it may be right that the branch should be cut away. Yes, that does happen.

The branch with some fruit

Here is a branch that is not all show; there is just a little fruit – not much to talk about, but a little. Is that your church, do you think? Some new Christians, a few clusters of grapes beginning to set? That is the way with most churches, I think. What may you expect from the heavenly gardener? *Every branch that does bear fruit he trims clean so that it will be even more fruitful.*

We may confidently look for the careful, loving hand of our Father at work among us, trimming and tending the branch so that it may yet become a significant part of the vine. Pruning is of course painful. We must expect it! *Do not be surprised at the painful trial you are suffering, as though something strange were happening to you,* says St Peter (1 Peter 4:12). Being turned into a fruitful branch is going to be an uncomfortable business. So don't be put off when Church life is difficult.

The good branch

What is the secret of the fully fruiting branch? How does it do it? It is all a question of how the branch relates to the vine. *No branch can bear fruit by itself; it must remain in the vine. Neither can you bear fruit unless you remain in me.* Here is the secret our Lord is trying to teach us. It all depends on our relationship with him. It is a *personal* thing for each one of us to get right; and a *corporate* thing for the whole Church community working together.

How are things between you and Christ? Is he a close companion of yours, or just a distant figurehead? It is all important for the health of the branch. The web of prayer to which you add your few threads, is it strong or full of holes? Do you come to worship with a heart tuned to Christ and expecting his touch? For it will affect us all when we come together.

There is a mystery in this inter-dependence of the Body and its relationship to Christ. But it is all very down-to-earth and practical; our Lord always is. *Apart from me you can do nothing.* It is on him that our fruitfulness depends.

Friday – Lent 3

What sort of garden?

> In those days when the number of disciples was increasing, the Grecian Jews among them complained against those of the Aramaic-speaking community because their widows were being overlooked in the daily distribution of food. So the Twelve gathered all the disciples together and said, 'It would not be right for us to neglect the ministry of the word of God in order to wait on tables. Brothers, choose seven men from among you who are known to be full of the Spirit and wisdom. We will turn this responsibility over to them and will give our attention to prayer and the ministry of the word.'
>
> This proposal pleased the whole group. They chose Stephen, a man full of faith and of the Holy Spirit; also Philip, Procorus, Nicanor, Timon, Parmenas, and Nicolas from Antioch, a convert to Judaism. They presented these men to the apostles, who prayed and laid their hands on them.
>
> So the word of God spread. The number of disciples in Jerusalem increased rapidly, and a large number of priests became obedient to the faith.   ACTS 6:1–7

Growth produces its own sorts of problems. How are the weeds doing in your flower beds? Keeping a garden in order can take a lot of time. One way of solving the problem is to lay the whole space down to concrete. No weeds, no gardening, no trouble! Some people wish the Church were like this – set for ever in stone and cement. They like the security of firm unchanging patterns. But this does not seem to be the way the Holy Spirit works.

In the garden nature has a marvellous way of planting new life in the cracks and crevices of even the most neatly laid patio. Left to itself nature is usually able to turn the most sterile man-made wilderness into a sort of jungle. The work of the Holy Spirit in the Church is often like this. He likes a Church with real life in it, with all the attendant dangers of wild growth and disorder. Problems of life he knows how to handle; with death and sterility his only problem is how to break it up. Ponder this if you are troubled by the many changes in Church life that our generation has seen. It is important in a time of change to have our priorities right.

Crisis in Jerusalem

Look how the early Church handled a crisis in its development. Alongside their programme of teaching, preaching, healing and fellowship they had set up a local care network to look after the poor and needy. At first the Apostles could handle the work themselves. However, the Church grew. It was supposed to! And the point came when the Aramaic-speaking Apostles failed to notice the needs of the Greek-speaking part of the congregation. There was tension in the Church and a feeling of rejection.

The Apostles are clear that their priority must be prayer and preaching. So they invite the congregation to choose seven people who could handle the administration. The congregation agree, and elect seven men with Greek names (presumably Greek-speaking). What a gracious, healing Christian act! – to trust their needs into the hands of those they had been at odds with! So the seven are commissioned by the Apostles.

The way of the Holy Spirit

But they could not have guessed what the Holy Spirit would do then. The seven were chosen for a job of administration. But the Holy Spirit used their work to open new doors for the Gospel. *The word of God spread, and the number of disciples in Jerusalem increased rapidly.* In the rest of chapter 6 and chapter 8 we read how two of the seven, Stephen and Philip, were used in special ways.

This is a familiar pattern in Church life. We have a management problem and appoint someone to cope with it. We then find that, as well as dealing with the problem, the Lord is using people in new and unexpected ways. You choose a verger, and find he has a ministry to strangers; you ask someone to deliver the magazines, and find she has a ministry to the lonely. You appoint an administrator, and find an evangelist. The Holy Spirit will help us with problems, but he also uses them creatively to produce new growth and development. If you are invited to help in the Church, do the job carefully; but the good Lord may have something else in mind too!

Do not shy away from the problems of life and growth – so much better than the problems of death! Keeping the garden in order may be a back-breaking job, and sometimes we wonder if it is worth it. But the results are often unexpected and quite delightful.

Saturday – Lent 3

Three loaves

> Then Jesus said to them, 'Suppose one of you has a friend, and he goes to him at midnight and says, "Friend, lend me three loaves of bread, because a friend of mine on a journey has come to me, and I have nothing to set before him."
>
> 'Then the one inside answers, "Don't bother me. The door is already locked, and my children are with me in bed. I can't get up and give you anything." I tell you, though he will not get up and give him the bread because he is his friend, yet because of the man's persistence he will get up and give him as much as he needs.'   LUKE 11:5–8

It is midnight, and suddenly a friend on a journey has called. He must be fed and sheltered, and sent on his way refreshed. But there is no food in the house. So the unwilling host hurries round to a neighbour to try and find the resources to meet his friend's need.

It is a very human little picture. And like all the parables of Jesus it speaks of a much deeper human need than just the problems of hospitality with an empty larder. It is part of a lesson Jesus gave his disciples on prayer. Here he is talking about prayer in one particular situation – a friend needs help urgently and we do not know what to say or do.

It might not have seemed important to the disciples at the time, but before long they were going to be in just such situations – St Peter ushered into a room full of gentiles (Cornelius's family and friends, Acts 10:25–end), feeling quite unprepared, as a Jew, for such a thing – St Paul cold, tired and battered in a Philippian jail (Acts 16:25–34), and suddenly an earthquake and the jailor is on his knees asking for help (and in this case it was actually midnight). This kind of thing is going to happen occasionally to every minister, as well as to any Christian who means to be available for the Lord to use. Before us is another person needing help, and we feel ill-equipped and wish we could put it off.

It is one of those moments when we really pray – an urgent cry from the heart. We are not ready, and do not deserve God's help; but unlike the neighbour in the parable he welcomes that desperate cry, and responds instantly. St Peter was not left to flounder, but was able to open up a whole new area of the community to the gospel. St Paul stammered out some hasty words to stop the jailor committing suicide, and added a whole new household to the growing Church. We have the same God as they; and we must be ready to do whatever he asks of us, at midnight, or whenever the challenge comes. He will not let us down.

But why THREE loaves? The meaning is plain enough in the ancient rules of hospitality. There is one loaf for our friend, one so that we may eat with him, and one more to prove there is no shortage. And this is the spiritual law. One for the other person, one for you, and in Jesus plenty to spare for all needs. We minister the grace of God to a friend, and suddenly find our own darkness of spirit lit up; and the good Lord is with us, and we know there is in him enough and to spare for a needy world.

Do you dare ask him to present YOU with challenges such as Peter and Paul faced – occasions when you will be forced to trust him to stand by you? Sometimes for good reasons God allows his children to experience a time of darkness, and then he presents them at 'midnight' with a challenge to bring spiritual help to someone else. Of course he has the resources to help you out; and you will meet the other person's need – and incidentally find your own spiritual darkness lifted.

> We beseech you, Lord, to guide your Church with your perpetual governance; that it may walk warily in times of quiet, and boldly in times of trouble; through Jesus Christ our Lord.
>
> *The Franciscan Breviary*
> *17th Century*

Discussion Starters – *3rd Week in Lent*

1. We are told to bring everything to God in prayer – everything that matters to us. How can we avoid being self-centred in our prayer life?

2. God himself is the answer to all our prayers. Does your experience illustrate this truth?

3. The united prayer of your church on a Sunday should be a real gathering up of your individual prayers through the week? How can you best achieve this?

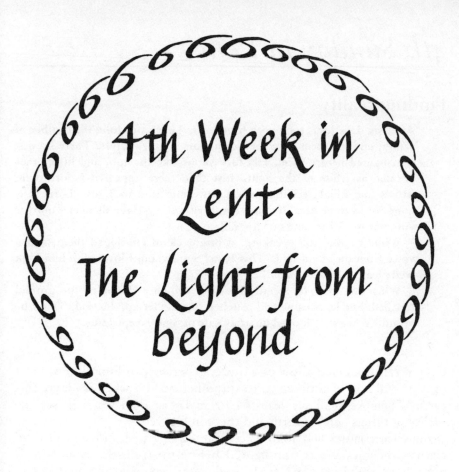

4th Week in Lent: The Light from beyond

PRESENT STRENGTH FROM ETERNITY

O gracious and holy Father, give us wisdom to see you, diligence to seek you, patience to wait for you, eyes to behold you, a heart to meditate upon you, and a life to proclaim you; through the power of the Spirit of Jesus Christ our Lord.

St Benedict
6th Century

4th Sunday in Lent

Finding reality

> After six days Jesus took with him Peter, James and John the brother of James, and led them up a high mountain by themselves. There he was transfigured before them. His face shone like the sun, and his clothes became as white as the light. Just then there appeared before them Moses and Elijah, talking with Jesus. Peter said to Jesus, 'Lord, it is good for us to be here. If you wish, I will put up three shelters – one for you, one for Moses and one for Elijah.'
>
> While he was still speaking, a bright cloud enveloped them, and a voice from the cloud said, 'This is my Son, whom I love, with him I am well pleased. Listen to him!'
>
> When the disciples heard this they fell face down to the ground terrified. But Jesus came and touched them. 'Get up,' he said. 'Don't be afraid.' When they looked up, they saw no-one except Jesus.
>
> MATTHEW 17:1–8

Only rarely does God allow us a direct experience of himself. For most of us it will not be until we go to stand before him when we leave this earth. Then we shall see Jesus as he really is; then we shall see the reality of things here on earth and there in Heaven.

But Peter, James and John were granted one such moment of total clarity when Jesus was transfigured before them on the mountain. It must have stabilised their faith, and left them believing in Jesus in quite a new way. It is often the same when people visit the Holy Land. They touch the Roman pavement on which Jesus stood before Pilate; they sit by the Sea of Galilee, and paddle their feet. And suddenly they say to themselves, 'Golly! It really happened!'

How important it is to see things as they really are. For the inner reality of things is often very different from their appearance. How was it for Peter and his friends on that mountain?

The reality of Jesus
They had already understood by faith who Jesus was. *You are the Christ, the Son of the living God*, Peter had cried out (Matthew 16:16). But that was not how it looked when their Companion was tired and dirty from long journeys on foot. On the mountain for the first time

they saw Jesus as he really is. They saw him radiant with the divine glory and receiving the worship of Heaven – then the voice from Heaven that announced him to be the Son of God. The experience was quite overwhelming, and they fell to the ground terrified. So would we if it happened to us.

The reality of Heaven

The important thing about Heaven is the presence of Jesus. Moses and Elijah had their whole attention on him; for he is the link between Earth and Heaven. He is the one who straddles Time and Eternity. On the mountain of Transfiguration it was all very clear. Heaven was real. Jesus was real. Earth was real too – don't we know it! But Jesus was Lord of it all.

The reality of the Church

There on the mountain the WHOLE Church was represented, the Old Testament Church by Moses and Elijah, the New by the Apostles. Moses was the great representative of tradition, the ancient tradition of the Jews. Elijah was the first of the prophets and the great innovator. Moses the traditionalist, Elijah the progressive, we might say. Peter wanted to hang on to them both, but he had to learn that only Jesus can unlock the future. *This is my Son . . . Listen to* HIM. Jesus alone can truly preserve and value the old, while at the same time creating the new.

The reality of the world

They could see the flesh of Jesus – human flesh, OUR flesh – shining with the life and glory of God. Thereafter every part of human life would seem important; for if Jesus dwelt within, it could glow with divine radiance. Even his clothes shone, garments that have long since decayed away. But they gained an eternal value by the presence of Jesus within them.

This is the truth by which things and people in this world are to be judged. Is Jesus there within them? Take a church or a person, a committee or a community, and just one question matters: Is Jesus there? At the end of his ministry our Lord finally walked away from the Temple that rejected him: *Your house is left to you desolate* (Matthew 23:38). How desolate without Jesus! But where Jesus is, there is new life and health. Everything is full of fresh creative possibilities. That is the inner reality of things in this world.

Monday – Lent 4

In light inaccessible

We did not follow cleverly invented stories when we told you about the power and coming of our Lord Jesus Christ, but we were eye-witnesses of his majesty. For he received honour and glory from God the Father when the voice came to him from the Majestic Glory, saying, 'This is my Son, whom I love; with him I am well pleased.' We ourselves heard this voice that came from heaven where we were with him on the sacred mountain.

And we have the word of the prophets made more certain, and you will do well to pay attention to it, as to a light shining in a dark place, until the day dawns and the morning star rises in your hearts.

2 PETER 1:16–19

We see a lot of cloudy weather in England. But have you ever thought what it would be like if our Earth was always totally covered with clouds (like the planet Venus)? Could we know there was a sun?

'This daylight comes from somewhere,' you might reason; 'there must be a big light up there above the clouds.' 'There's no big light,' others would say; 'it's just the clouds themselves that are luminous during the daytime; the light comes from them.'

At the seaside we would observe the twice-daily movement of the tides. 'Up there above the clouds,' you might say, 'there must be some great object that causes this heaving of our oceans.' 'That's a clever idea,' we reply. But we would not believe you! In any case what does it matter? Theories! Theories! Meanwhile life must go on.

Then one day a report comes from a distant land of three men on a mountain expedition: 'We sat down to rest. And suddenly the clouds parted above our heads, and there it was – a great shining white light, too bright to look at – and all around it the sky was brilliant *blue*.' How the world would put those men and their story to the test! For most of us, however, it would remain an unlikely tale, to be dismissed as a clever hoax or a wild fantasy.

When Jesus moved about among men, his glory was hidden. His body, like clouds about him, kept the light of his presence to a tolerable level. His close friends eventually guessed that the power of his life and words came from heaven. But others said: 'He is a good man. That is all.' For centuries the upheaval caused by his brief stay on Earth has made people stop and wonder. But most find it hard to believe in him.

Just once on the mountain of Transfiguration the glory of Jesus was allowed to shine through. For a few brief minutes Peter, James and John saw the Son of God as he really is. And then, as suddenly, the clouds closed around him again and the glory was concealed until the conclusion of his great battle against the forces of darkness.

For St Peter the Transfiguration was a transforming experience; it altered his whole view of things; and this he tries to share with us. He wants us to know that the reality we cannot see is the important thing; while the facade of the material world that dominates our senses is only the protective shield to save us from having to face too much reality all at once. And so we have a free choice whether to seek the light or not.

One day we shall be exposed to the full light of his presence, and that should be for us a moment of joy and fulfilment, not of fear and terror. But there will be some who will prefer the outer darkness, where the clouds for ever hide from the presence of God.

With so much depending on it, no wonder the world put those early disciples to the test! Almost all the Apostles died as martyrs. But their testimony still rings as true as a bell.

Tuesday – Lent 4

Is it true?

> Now, brothers, I want to remind you of the gospel I preached to you,
> which you received and on which you have taken your stand . . . For
> what I received I passed on to you as of first importance: that Christ
> died for our sins according to the Scriptures, that he was buried, that he
> was raised on the third day according to the Scriptures, and that he
> appeared to Peter, and then to the Twelve. After that, he appeared to
> more than five hundred of the brothers at the same time, most of whom
> are still living, though some have fallen asleep. Then he appeared to
> James, then to all the apostles, and last of all he appeared to me also, as
> to one abnormally born. . . . Whether, then, it was I or they, this is
> what we preach, and this is what you believed.
>
> But if it is preached that Christ has been raised from the dead, how
> can some of you say that there is no resurrection of the dead? If there is
> no resurrection of the dead, then not even Christ has been raised. And if
> Christ has not been raised, our preaching is useless and so is your faith.
> More than that, we are then found to be false witnesses about God, for
> we have testified about God that he raised Christ from the dead. But he
> did not raise him if in fact the dead are not raised. For if the dead are
> not raised, then Christ has not been raised either. And if Christ has not
> been raised, your faith is futile; you are still in your sins. Then those
> also who have fallen asleep in Christ are lost. If only for this life we
> have hope in Christ, we are to be pitied more than all men.
>
> But Christ has indeed been raised from the dead, the first fruits of
> those who have fallen asleep.   1 CORINTHIANS 15:1–20

There is only one question that really matters about the Christian
Faith, namely: IS IT TRUE? And this is the same as asking: Did Jesus
Christ rise from the dead? For if that happened then everything else
follows. If it did not – then, in St Paul's words, *our preaching is
useless, and so is your faith*; and we as Christians *are to be pitied more
than all men*. How absurd to be following a delusion – if that is what
it is! But how absurd to be ignoring the resurrection of Jesus, if *that* is
what happened! So the evidence deserves to be looked at, does it not?
Be scientific about it.

I love the story of Galileo, one of the founders of modern science, after he had invented the telescope. They persecuted him because he asserted that the Earth goes round the Sun. He had turned his new telescope on the planet Jupiter and discovered a whole system of moons going round it, just like a miniature solar system. He wrote about it to his great friend Johannes Kepler (who was eventually to find the laws governing planetary motion):

My dear Kepler,
If only you could see the Professor of Astronomy at Pisa, trying to charm my new planets out of the sky by his arguments. I have invited him to come and look through my telescope but he REFUSES . . .

What a laugh! It was too uncomfortable to face the evidence, so he refused even to look at it. He goes down in history as one of the most ridiculous characters. Don't be like that poor old professor. Look at the evidence. DID JESUS RISE FROM THE DEAD? It stands up to the closest scrutiny. It will certainly turn your world upside down when you find that he did. But don't refuse even to look!

It may be unfashionable to believe in Jesus Christ. Galileo's view were unfashionable too. But who was right? I feel in good company, for with the Apostles and with the whole Church down the centuries I am quite sure that Jesus Christ rose from the dead. Incidentally, Galileo and Kepler both believed that too.

Wednesday – Lent 4

The pivot of history

The people walking in darkness have seen a great light;
  on those living in the land of the shadow of death
    a light has dawned. . . .
For to us a child is born, to us a son is given,
  and the government will be on his shoulders.
And he will be called Wonderful Counsellor, Mighty God,
  Everlasting Father, Prince of Peace.
Of the increase of his government and peace
  there will be no end.
He will reign on David's throne and over his kingdom,
  establishing and upholding it with justice and righteousness
  from that time on and for ever.
The zeal of the Lord Almighty will accomplish this.   ISAIAH 9:2,6–7

Mass communications and the growth of knowledge have made catastrophes seem commonplace. Twenty thousand die in an earthquake, and in hours the whole world knows about it. So our mental picture of the world is one in which we seem to lurch from one crisis to the next. History and Science alike emphasise it. We read of the awful things men have done to each other in the past; and the grisly record seems endless. And Geology points to past upheavals more terrible than anything we have known.

But closer reflection shows that the real life of the world develops on the small scale. You would have needed a strong microscope to see anything at all when life first emerged in our oceans; and the steps of change that led to great creatures like the dinosaurs were always imperceptible. Human history is the same. Kings and their armies march hither and thither, and make a lot of noise. But the things that change the way we think and live happen quietly in the lives of individuals and communities.

The greatest event in human history was apparently very ordinary. A young mother in a small village gave birth to her first child; what is so special about that? (Ask any young mother, and she will tell you!) But this birth was unique. For there at Bethlehem the eternal God, the Creator of it all, was entering his own creation to perform the creative act that finally gave meaning and purpose to everything. Here is a script that requires the Playright himself to take the stage. In this symphony there is a line the Composer himself must play.

The birth of Jesus Christ was indeed the pivot of history. Everything before it led up to it. Everything since has depended on it. The world now lives (or dies) in relation to Jesus Christ. In the language of St John: *The Word became flesh and lived for a while among us* (John 1:14). And now everything is different.

The Greek philosophers saw the world as in danger of being engulfed in the primeval chaos – fearlessly they faced the thought. Before Jesus this world and the things in it were all that could be known for sure. Enjoy it while you can, for there may be nothing beyond, said the Greek philosophers. If there is a God who controls it, he is a remote unknowable being, they went on.

But now all this is changed. The apparent chaos we see as part of a mind-bending plan in the heart of the Creator; and the world is travelling towards a wonderful destiny. This life is not the limit of our experience; for heaven and earth have met at Bethlehem, bound together in one reality for ever in Jesus. If we belong to him we are heirs of both. So this world is important, and everything in it. Man is not just another species on the way to extinction, but a being of great significance. For the Creator was able to reveal himself in a human life; and the resurrection showed all human life as capable of being refashioned into a form fit for eternity.

Best of all, we find that our God is not remote but homely, and loves to reveal himself in the small human situation. Our loves and joys, our fears and the pressures upon us are the stuff he rejoices to share. The comings and goings of family life are the ingredients with which he creates a world. When the Son of God entered human life at Bethlehem a new world came into being. When he enters your life and becomes part of your family you enter a new world, one that he rules. Time and eternity are fused into one; eternal life – a new *quality* of life – begins now; the life of the world to come already infuses your life here and now.

Thursday – Lent 4

The herald of dawn

'Behold, I am coming soon! My reward is with me, and I will give to everyone according to what he has done. I am the Alpha and the Omega, the First and the Last, the Beginning and the End.

'Blessed are those who wash their robes, that they may have the right to the tree of life and may go through the gates into the city. Outside are the dogs, those who practise magic arts, the sexually immoral, the murderers, the idolaters and everyone who loves and practises falsehood.

'I, Jesus, have sent my angel to give you this testimony for the churches. I am the Root and the Offspring of David, and the bright Morning Star.'

The Spirit and the bride say, 'Come!' And let him who hears say, 'Come.' Whoever is thirsty, let him come; and whoever wishes, let him take the free gift of the water of life.   REVELATION 22:12-17

On the closing page of the Bible our Lord Jesus describes himself in a series of vivid symbols: Alpha and Omega, First and Last, Beginning and End. We do not live in a universe at the mercy of impersonal and fearful forces. The cosmos owes its origin to him and takes its character from him. Its ultimate meaning and destiny are to be found in him, and so is all the path it will take in arriving there. But then he goes on to use symbols of a more human kind.

He is the Root
St John had written: *Through him all things were made; without him nothing was made that has been made. In him was life, and that life was the light of men* (John 1:3-4). He is the Root of Man, the one who determined the character and qualities of Man. We are not at the mercy of dark forces in our own nature. By whatever mysterious path Mankind emerged on this planet, there is an inner pressure in the universe that drives evolution forward to yield a living being able to know its Creator and be like him.

The Offspring of David
He has entered the life of this world, and become part of his own

creation. He was born into the human race, at a particular time, in a particular way, and in a particular family – namely, the descendants of King David. He belongs to us all for ever. By his life and death and resurrection he has made it possible for us all to know God and be like him. In knowing our Lord Jesus, we find the way to *wash our robes* and we learn how to handle the evil pressures that so easily engulf us.

The Bright Morning Star

This was the name they gave to the planet Venus, the brightest object in the night sky (apart from the Moon). Venus, as we know, is in an orbit closer to the Sun than ourselves; and so it is always near the Sun in the sky. When the Morning Star shines the Sun is never far away. For people without clocks it was the herald of the dawn and the new day. It was the Star whose rising was full of promise and new hope.

We may have atomic clocks that split the second into billions of accurately measured parts. But I do not think we know what time it is in God's great purpose for his world. *The night is nearly over; the day is almost here*, wrote St Paul (Romans (13:12). How did he know? Because, for him as for us, the Morning Star is shining brightly in the heavens, and the LORD is close at hand.

I am coming soon, the Lord says. The New Testament is full of the promise (or for some, the *threat*) of the second coming of our Lord Jesus Christ to this earth. The fashion of the 20th Century is to ignore this teaching. Because we cannot imagine what form the second coming will take – and let's face it, we cannot! – we are not entitled therefore to deny it. Nobody could have guessed the form his first coming to this world would take either! What is quite clear is that history moves forward to a consummation in which the Lord Jesus will be central, as he has always been.

To be prepared for this is an urgent matter, for we do not now how much longer we have; it depends what God means by *soon*. This is not a threat but a promise, full of hope and love; it is part of a wonderful and generous offer of life – *Whoever is thirsty . . . whoever wishes . . . take the free gift of the water of life* – from Jesus, of course.

Friday – Lent 4

The colour of heaven

I heard behind me a loud voice like a trumpet, which said: 'Write on a scroll what you see and send it to the seven churches: . . .

I turned round to see the voice that was speaking to me. And when I turned I saw seven golden lampstands, and among the lampstands was someone 'like a son of man', dressed in a robe reaching down to his feet and with a golden sash round his chest. His head and hair were white like wool, as white as snow, and his eyes were like blazing fire. His feet were like bronze glowing in a furnace, and his voice was like the sound of rushing waters. In his right hand he held seven stars, and out of his mouth came a sharp double-edged sword. His face was like the sun shining in all its brilliance.

When I saw him, I fell at his feet as though dead. Then he placed his right hand on me and said: 'Do not be afraid. I am the First and the Last. I am the Living One; I was dead, and behold I am alive for ever and ever! And I hold the keys of death and Hades.' REVELATION 1:10–18

The death and resurrection of our Lord Jesus Christ revealed a way of doing things that is special to our God. First Christ died; then he rose to new life. If was not just the old life again, but a completely new sort of life, without the physical limitations of his former life, and suited to eternity.

The renewal of life every spring follows the same pattern. First there is a sort of dying; then life rises from the old – the same, yet new and always different. Nothing is wasted; what seems to die and be lost is actually used again.

More striking than this is the renewing work of the Holy Spirit in human lives and communities. God's way is so different from Man's. Man discards things and people when he has no further use for them, and creates rubbish tips and slums. God is able to make new life rise from the old, and the new is then a fresh creative act built on the roots of the old. The rising of the Church on the Day of Pentecost from its old Jewish roots is a case in point. It was a new thing, and yet marvellously continuous with the old.

It is the same with each one of us. We shall all die of course. And before that we shall find old age to be a sort of dying with which the

Lord graciously prepares us. Apart from that, every Lent is also meant to be a kind of dying, so that new life can emerge in ways that were not possible before. Eventually, when we go to be with Christ, we are promised risen bodies like his, with no physical limitations, and suitable for eternity.

'What's the colour of that rose?' asked the blind man.

'Bright yellow,' I replied.

'What is that like?' he said after a pause.

I fumbled for words. How could I explain such a thing to a man who had always been blind? 'It's rather like the sound of a trumpet,' I offered. He looked puzzled. 'I suppose you mean that it's very vivid,' he mused. 'The sort of colour you couldn't mistake.'

'It's rather like trying to describe heaven,' I went on. 'In the book of Revelation it's full of trumpets and strange beasts and bright things like jewels and rainbows. Difficult to know what it all means.'

'And I suppose we couldn't understand it even if we did have words to describe it,' he said.

'Then one day we shall open our eyes and see reality – heaven – for the first time.'

'What do you think will be the first thing we'll see?'

'I know the answer to that question,' I replied. 'We shall see Jesus. That is the one thing you can be sure of from the Bible descriptions. He'll be there to meet us.'

He thought for a bit. 'His voice is like the sound of a trumpet, it says in Revelation.'

'The sort of voice you couldn't mistake,' I quoted back at him. 'And then further on it says that his voice is like the sound of rushing waters.'

'That's rather frightening,' he frowned.

'Some people will find it so,' I said. 'Probably all of us will a little – even St John did!'

We stayed silent for a while. 'But that was the voice that raised the dead,' he said.

'And made the blind see,' I added.

'Yes,' he smiled; 'I can't wait.'

Saturday – Lent 4

It's lovely in

'Do not let your hearts be troubled. Trust in God; trust also in me. In my Father's house are many rooms; if it were not so, I would have told you. I am going there to prepare a place for you. And if I go and prepare a place for you, I will come back and take you to be with me that you also may be where I am. You know the way to the place where I am going.'

Thomas said to him, 'Lord, we don't know where you are going, so how can we know the way?'

Jesus answered, 'I am the way and the truth and the life. No-one comes to the Father except through me.'   JOHN 14:1–6

He came back from the beach with tousled hair, a towel over one arm and wet trunks hanging limply from his thumb. He looked so young and strong, and seemed enormously refreshed. His eyes shone as he stood before the rest of us huddled in the lounge of the guest-house. 'It's lovely in,' he said.

We laughed in disbelief; for it was still early in the season and the air was keen on the sea front, the water grey and forbidding. But secretly we all wished we had the young man's energy and vitality. It probably was much warmer in the water. But who else would be brave enough to find out?

It was like this that our Lord Jesus Christ came back to visit us from beyond the grave. The disciples were huddled in the upper room, shocked and appalled by the fate that had overtaken their Master. Death, it seemed, was the ultimate ruler of their lives, the unavoidable destroyer of all hopes and joys. Then suddenly Jesus was there among them. No apparition, this, but real and triumphant, showing up death for what it is – an unseemly interlude in our forward progress.

Many people tell me they find Easter a rather sad time. It revives memories of loved ones lost, and stirs afresh the poignancy of bereavement. And it reminds us again of our own mortality. The waters of death break incessantly on the shores of our lives; and we dread the plunge that sooner or later we must take. And so we huddle closer together, and try and avoid thinking about it.

How important it is that we come to terms with death, if we are to live our lives here and now to the full. I know no way of doing this except through the Easter victory of our Lord Jesus Christ. It is not just proof of survival that we need, or even the assurance of heaven at the end of the day. We need to know that the life we live now is part of a glorious plan that will find its fulfilment and completion in eternity. This is what Jesus has won for us; and to assure us of this he brings us even now, through the means of grace, a first instalment of his own risen life and power. Only those who are tasting the new life in Christ are able to live truly in the light of the Easter victory.

Jesus has come back from the grave in all the vigour of his risen life. '*Why are you troubled?*' he says (Luke 24:38). 'I have prepared a place for you. I will come back and take you to be with me. Meanwhile I offer you eternal life – even now – and a share in my unbounded joy – even now. So live your life, even now, to the full, for I promise that all things are going to work together for your good, come what may; and I will fulfil it all one day in my presence. Trust me with your life now and in eternity. I've got everything ready for you. I'll be there to meet you, and if you can't swim I'll hold you up. Don't be scared. It's lovely in.'

> Lord, lift up the light of your countenance upon us, that in your light we may see light: the light of your grace today, and the light of your glory hereafter; through Jesus Christ our Lord.
>
> *Bishop Lancelot Andrewes*
> *17th Century*

Discussion Starters – 4th Week in Lent

1. The Resurrection of Christ ought to silence all doubts and quieten all fears. But of course it is not as simple as that! How can we help each other when faith is hard?

2. If the coming into this world of the Son of God was the pivot on which human history turns, two things might follow from it:
   (a) a steady receding of the tide of evil in the world;

(b) a growth of evil towards some awful climax.
Can you perceive these things happening in the history of our world?

3. The Lord Jesus Christ used physical things as vehicles for spiritual reality. His incarnation in a human body was just that. How did he work out this principle in his method of teaching and in the way he set up his Church as a human institution working with Sacraments and a Bible?

5th Week in Lent: In the dark Valley

FIGHTING THE GOOD FIGHT

O Eternal Lord God, who holds all souls in life: we ask you to shed forth upon your whole Church in Paradise and on Earth the bright beams of your light and heavenly comfort; and grant that we, following the good example of those who have served you here and are at rest, may at the last enter with them into the fullness of your unending joy; through Jesus Christ our Lord.

Bishop John Wordsworth
20th Century

5th Sunday in Lent

They want to see Jesus

Now there were some Greeks among those who went up to worship at the Feast. They came to Philip, . . . 'Sir,' they said, 'we would like to see Jesus.' Philip went to tell Andrew; Andrew and Philip in turn told Jesus.

Jesus replied, 'The hour has come for the Son of Man to be glorified. I tell you the truth, unless an ear of wheat falls to the ground and dies, it remains only a single seed. But if it dies, it produces many seeds. The man who loves his life will lose it, while the man who hates his life in this world will keep it for eternal life. Whoever serves me must follow me; and where I am, my servant also will be. My Father will honour the one who serves me.

'Now my heart is troubled, and what shall I say? "Father, save me from this hour?" No, it was for this very reason I came to this hour. Father, glorify your name! . . . Now is the time for judgment on this world; now the prince of this world will be driven out. But I, when I am lifted up from the earth, will draw all men to myself.'   JOHN 12:20–32

We Christians are no longer surprised by the truth that Christ had to die. It was devastating for those first disciples, but not for us; 2000 years is long enough to get used to the idea. We see clearly enough that this grain of wheat had to fall to the ground and die if there was to be a rich harvest. But the Lord Jesus goes on and extends the principle to the lives of all his followers, and that surprises us greatly. The ear of wheat that seeks to be kept as it is, admired and treasured, will stay solitary and lifeless, and miss its true destiny. Only the seed that falls to the ground and is lost in the earth has a future.

We mean to be true followers of Christ; we would like the world to see Jesus through us; and we hope to fulfil our calling in his service. But here is a hard word. For it seems that to do this we must *hate* our lives in this world, and that sounds unbalanced. Like all difficult points of Christian teaching it can be understood only through the life and example of our Lord Jesus Christ. In him it was worked out to perfection. In his hands this is no negative teaching.

He enjoyed his work
Our Lord is not calling us to renounce all joys and pleasures. He

enjoyed the good things of life when it was right to have them. In particular he enjoyed his work. I am sure he loved preaching and telling stories. Healing people must have given him profound satisfaction. He could have avoided the cross and gone on doing this, deeply respected and admired into a ripe old age. But that would have been to love his life, and so lose what he came into the world to do. More important to him than his work was the will of his Father; when God required it everything, even life itself, was to be laid aside. He shrank from death, but was prepared for it if his Father called him to it. He loved life, and lived it to the full. But more important was the will of his Father. So he fulfilled his calling, and entered into life eternal for us all.

The Christian vocation

If you have a clear vocation in life, you will certainly find much joy and satisfaction in fulfilling it. But if the Lord requires it, you must be prepared for times when it will bring you only sorrow and trouble, and you must be ready at his bidding cheerfully to lay it aside altogether. Only so will you fulfil your calling and find your true destiny in Christ. If your objective is satisfaction in your work, you will miss your true vocation – though you may well live out your days deeply respected and admired. Seek satisfaction and you lose all; follow the path laid out by the good Lord, and you will incidentally find much satisfaction and lasting joy.

The world around us comes to us, his disciples, with an unspoken request to see Jesus. So they will, if we dwell in him and the will of God is more important to us than life itself. They look to us, not for good advice, but with a dim perception that in Jesus they might see their questions answered. Those Greeks had come at the right moment. The hour had come. They were about to witness the key event of human history. All their questions would be answered, if they stayed around and looked. When he was lifted from the earth at Calvary, they too would be irresistibly drawn to him.

So we are called to lift up Christ, by our preaching, by our liturgy, by the celebration of our life in Christ. But if the world is to see him in us and be drawn to him, it will only be as we take up our cross and follow him in the path he marked out so clearly.

Monday – Lent 5

A lamb to the slaughter

He was despised and rejected by men,
  a man of sorrows, and familiar with suffering.
Like one from whom men hide their faces
  he was despised, and we esteemed him not.
Surely he took up our infirmities
  and carried our sorrows,
yet we considered him stricken by God,
  smitten by him, and afflicted.
But he was pierced for our transgressions,
  he was crushed for our iniquities;
the punishment that brought us peace was upon him,
  and by his wounds we are healed.
We all, like sheep, have gone astray,
  each of us has turned to his own way;
and the Lord has laid on him
  the iniquity of us all.
He was oppressed and afflicted,
  yet he did not open his mouth;
he was led like a lamb to the slaughter,
  and as a sheep before her shearers is silent,
  so he did not open his mouth.
By oppression and judgement,
  he was taken away.
  And who can speak of his descendents?
For he was cut off from the land of the living;
  for the transgression of my people he was stricken.
He was assigned a grave with the wicked,
  and with the rich in his death,
though he had done no violence,
  nor was any deceit in his mouth. . . .
For he bore the sin of many,
  and made intercession for the trangressors.   ISAIAH 53:3–12

We need to realise that the cross is an eternal event. It was also a real event in this world; for it happened at a particular place (on Calvary outside Jerusalem), as a particular time (when Pontius Pilate governed

Judea), and to a particular person (namely Jesus the carpenter of Nazareth). But the one who died was also an eternal being, the Son of God. Therefore the suffering and death of Jesus on the cross is also an eternal event. And that is another way of saying that it is *always* present and for ever real in its effects. The same applies of course to his resurrection; the risen life he won for us is an ever-present reality that he shares with us.

The accounts of the resurrection emphasise this point. When our Lord met his disciples on Easter evening, *he showed them his hands and his side.* (John 20:20) And the following week to Thomas, *Put your finger here; see my hands. Reach out your hand and put it into my side. Stop doubting and believe.* (John 20:27) Although his body was transformed and glorified, the nail wounds and the spear thrust are wounds he carries with him in eternity.

The book of Revelation makes the same point in its own symbolic way: *Then I saw a Lamb, looking as if it had been slain, standing in the centre of the throne.* (Revelation 5:6) And later it refers to him as *the Lamb that was slain from the creation of the world.* (Revelation 13:8) Our Lord is for ever the bearer of our sin, as well as of our sorrow and suffering; just as he is for ever the source of new life.

There is an eternal gash in the heart of the Godhead where the unbearable is borne and carried away. The spear thrust in his side was its sacramental expression. Our sin and suffering strike directly into the heart of God, and nothing is reflected back to add to this world's troubles. From that wound flows only the crimson flood that cleanses and heals. It is a mystery of love we shall never really see into. This is the spiritual truth that thrilled the prophets and which they were always sensing and seeking to describe. Nowhere is this done more beautifully than in Isaiah's lovely poem on the Passion. Why not read it again?

Tuesday – Lent 5

All shall be well

> We know that in all things God works for the good of those who love him, who have been called according to his purpose. For those God foreknew he also predestined to be conformed to the likeness of his Son, that he might be the firstborn among many brothers. . . .
>
> What, then, shall we say in response to this? If God is for us, who can be against us? He who did not spare his own Son, but gave him up for us all – how will he not also, along with him, graciously give us all things? Who will bring any charge against those whom God has chosen? It is God who justifies. Who is he that condemns? Christ Jesus, who died – more than that, who was raised to life – is at the right hand of God and is also interceding for us. Who shall separate us from the love of Christ?   ROMANS 8:28–35

You must have heard the famous saying of Mother Julian of Norwich: '*All shall be well, and all shall be well, and all manner of thing shall be well.*' It is an insight granted to the human spirit at its most simple and childlike. The same insight thrilled St Paul as he asserted the ability of God to carry forward his loving purposes in the face of every obstacle raised by human frailty and worldly pressures. WE KNOW, he asserts – the sort of knowing that comes from long-tested experience. This knowledge may be yours too.

In all things God works for good
He allows no room for exceptions. With the good things of life we can all believe it. But when things go wrong, it is much harder. With loss and bereavement, weakness and failure, with difficult people and impossible pressures – what then? Is God at work in these things too? YES, says St Paul, and he speaks from a personal knowledge of imprisonments and beatings, shipwreck and danger, treachery and false dealing, and every deprivation known to man. IN ALL THINGS, he says, with the confident voice of experience. Behind all the chaos of our lives God's power is at work to fulfil his good purposes for us.

We see this supremely in the cross. God allows it; but thereby he draws for ever the poison of evil and the sting of death. Our Lord always focusses on his Father's love and will. In Gethsemane he looks beyond the evil and refers to *the cup the* FATHER *has given me*. (John 18:11) To Pilate he says: '*You would have no power over me if it were not given to you* FROM ABOVE.' (John 19:11) He ignores the injustice and cruelty, and focusses on his Father's love.

Who does it apply to?

St Paul's statement applied to *those who love God, who have been called according to his purpose*. Does this apply to you?

(a) **Do you love God?** I hope your response is not too brash. Remember what Simon Peter answered when Jesus asked him, *Do you love me?* 'Yes, Lord,' he said. '*You know that I love you.*' (John 21:15–16) Good theology, Peter! Far better to rely on the clear knowledge of the Lord Jesus, than to trust your own limited perception of your motives. It does not matter what your *feelings* about God may be. What matters is what your actions say.

(b) **Have you been called?** Oh dear, you say, I have never heard the call of God. But let me put the question another way. Are you in the place God wants you? If you are, then you have been called according to his purpose. You may never have heard his call simply because you are already just where he wants you. However, if you know that you have departed from the path where the Lord Jesus protects and guides, or if you fear you have somehow missed the way, then you must repent and seek the way back. Do you suppose there is no longer any welcome for prodigals who return? You know the Lord better than that.

But St Paul is writing for those who are perplexed and just do not know what to think and believe, as the pressures pile up in their lives. If that is your situation, take heart. For the Apostle assures you that even this dark time of yours is being fashioned by the loving creative hand of our God into a good that will leave you speechless. St Paul knew it in his damp and lonely prison in Rome, and you may know it in the cell of your circumstances. Mother Julian knew it in her 14th Century anchorite cell, which I do not suppose was any more comfortable than St Paul's or yours. She could not tear herself away from the lovely thought – *All shall be well, . . . and all shall be well, . . . and all manner of thing shall be well*. I know it too, and so may you.

Wednesday – Lent 5

Five smooth stones

Goliath stood and shouted to the ranks of Israel, 'Why do you come out and line up for battle? Am I not a Philistine, and are you not the servants of Saul? Choose a man and have him come down to me. If he is able to fight and kill me, we will become your subjects; but if I overcome him and kill him, you will become our subjects and serve us.' On hearing the Philistine's words Saul and all the Israelites were dismayed and terrified. . . . For forty days the Philistine came forward every morning and evening and took his stand. . . .

David said to Saul, 'Let no-one lose heart on account of this Philistine; your servant will go and fight him.'

Saul replied, 'You are not able to go out against this Philistine and fight him; you are only a boy, and he has been a fighting man from his youth.'

But David said to Saul, 'Your servant has been keeping his father's sheep. When a lion or a bear came and carried off a sheep from the flock, I went after it, struck it and rescued the sheep from its mouth. When it turned on me, I seized it by its hair, struck it and killed it. . . . this uncircumcised Philistine will be like one of them, because he has defied the armies of the living God. The Lord who delivered me from the paw of the lion and paw of the bear will deliver me from the hand of this Philistine.'

Saul said to David, 'Go, and the Lord be with you.' Then Saul dressed David in his own tunic. He put a coat of armour on him and a bronze helmet on his head. David fastened on his sword over the tunic and tried walking around, because he was not used to them.

'I cannot go in these,' he said to Saul, 'because I am not used to them.' So he took them off. Then he took his staff in his hand, chose five smooth stones from the stream, put them in the pouch of his shepherd's bag and, with his sling in his hand, approached the Philistine. Meanwhile, the Philistine, with his shield-bearer in front of him, kept coming closer to David. He looked David over and saw that he was only a boy, ruddy and handsome, and he . . . cursed David by his gods. 'Come here,' he said, 'and I'll give your flesh to the birds of the air and the beasts of the field!'

David said to the Philistine, 'You come against me with sword and spear and javelin, but I come against you in the name of the Lord

Almighty, the God of the armies of Israel, whom you have defied. This day the Lord will hand you over to me, . . . and the whole world will know that there is a God in Israel. . . .

As the Philistine moved closer to attack him, David ran quickly towards the battle line to meet him. Reaching into his bag and taking out a stone, he slung it and struck the Philistine on the forehead. The stone sank into his forehead, and he fell face down on the ground. So David triumphed over the Philistine with a sling and a stone; without a sword in his hand he struck down the Philistine and killed him.

1 SAMUEL 17:8–16 & 32–50

So the small plucky hero defeats the loud-mouthed bully – the little man with righteousness on his side against the overbearing tyrant who deals in lies and fear. It is a favourite sort of story; and the Bible has many examples – for God often calls people to go out and battle against oppression and evil. And God has his own way of preparing such people. Let us look at David's example.

1. **David's obedience to his God.** Saul was demoralised by disobedience. He knew he had not gone God's way. So did his army. So he could have no confidence that God would be with him. You can only be sure of God when you are where he wants you.

2. **David's desert training.** The desert is a tough and lonely place with many dangers, where no-one but God knows what you do. But in the desert you prove the Lord's protection, and God becomes real. Do not fear the desert experience if you want to be used by God.

3. **David's shepherd-heart.** He had learnt how to care for his flock. Later, as king, he would care for his people like this. God's servant cannot rest while they are enslaved by any 'Goliath'.

4. **David's ambition for his God.** As he went out he wanted the whole world to know there was a God in Israel. David believed in a living God who intervenes in this world's affairs.

5. **David won the Lord's way.** Saul gave him the usual armour. But David laid it all aside, and took just the staff and sling God had taught him to use. God's battles are to be fought God's way – which is the way we see in Jesus.

Five smooth stones, smooth because well worn by the rush of water in the stream – just as God's way has been well tested in the experience of his people. It is the only way you and I will win.

Thursday – Lent 5

The call of God

> The word of the Lord came to me, saying, 'Before I formed you in the womb I knew you, before you were born I set you apart; I appointed you as a prophet to the nations.'
>
> 'Ah, Sovereign Lord,' I said, 'I do not know how to speak; I am only a child.' But the Lord said to me, 'Do not say, "I am only a child." You must go to everyone I send you to and say whatever I command you. Do not be afraid of them, for I am with you and will rescue you,' declares the Lord.
>
> Then the Lord reached out his hand and touched my mouth and said to me, 'Now, I have put my words in your mouth. See, today I appoint you over nations and kingdoms to uproot and tear down, to destroy and overthrow, to build and to plant.'   JEREMIAH 1:4–10

You and I are not called, I think, to be *prophets to the nations*; indeed no-one has ever been called to do Jeremiah's work – except Jeremiah. But then, no-one has ever been called to do your work – except you! So it is just the same, and the same principles apply. What are they?

Appointed before he was born

What a staggering thought! Before we were born God chose us for the work we were to do. This applies to all Christians. In the words of St Paul: *We are God's workmanship, created in Christ Jesus to do good works, which God prepared in advance for us to do.* (Ephesians 2:10) This is called *predestination*, if you want a pompous word – the truth that our God sees the end from the beginning. And always in Scripture this is balanced beside the truth of the *free-will* of Man.

But think first of the God who has detailed foreknowledge of us and all our works. We need this doctrine. For it assures us that God does not make mistakes. He chose you and me, knowing full well all our failings and mistakes, and seeing precisely all the circumstances that would bedevil out lives. He knew what he was doing when he chose us. We also need this doctrine to protect our church fellowship. He chose you as much as he chose me; and if we should get on each other's nerves, this is all amongst the things he has foreseen and allowed for, and we must accept it. We are all chosen and special, and no one is to be edged out as inadequate or a mistake. It is a useful doctrine.

A sense of unworthiness
I do not know how to speak; I am only a child. Poor Jeremiah! He was perhaps a tongue-tied 16-year-old at this point, with no experience in public speaking, and no idea what to say. It is always so when God calls us to do a job. It seems impossible; and this is a healthy reaction up to a point, if we see clearly what is involved.

But God re-assures Jeremiah: *I have put my words in your mouth.* A prophet needs words, and he got them. Whatever we *need* for our work we will receive – though not perhaps what we *think* we need. Jeremiah may have thought he needed success. But he was a terrible failure. No-one believed his prophecies – not until long after he was dead. But strangely and wonderfully, as *we* can see, the purposes of God were moved forward by Jeremiah's work.

Worked out in obedience
You must go to everyone I send you to, and say whatever I command you. The call is to obedience. *We have been chosen according to the foreknowledge of God the Father, . . . for obedience to Jesus Christ . . .* (1 Peter 1:2) I said that God's foreknowledge is balanced in Scripture beside Man's free will. So it is. God's choice – our choice. Both are free. Impossible! says logic. If God knows it all ahead, how can we be free? But life says otherwise, in a paradox deeper than logic. It is what St Paul calls *the glorious freedom of the children of God.* (Romans 8:21) We are called to respond to God in loving obedience, who sets us free to be entirely what we were meant to be – and what in the end we most want.

There will be much to oppose our discipleship, within ourselves and in the world. *But do not be afraid of them, for I am with you and will rescue you.* The God who called us has the measure of it all; he is with us and not a hair of our heads shall perish. Jeremiah became one of the architects of that great rebuilding of the life of his nation, that carried them forward to the time of our Lord. His contribution was unique and vital. So it is with you and me. God chose us, even us, to be links in the same chain Jeremiah helped to forge. It is an astounding privilege.

Friday – Lent 5

Cheerful giving

And now, brothers, we want you to know about the grace that God has given the Macedonian churches. Out of the most severe trial, their overflowing joy and their extreme poverty welled up in rich generosity. For I testify that they gave as much as they were able, and even beyond their ability. Entirely on their own, they urgently pleaded with us for the privilege of sharing in this service to the saints. And they did not do as we expected, but they gave themselves first to the Lord and then to us in keeping with God's will. . . .

I am not commanding you, but I want to test the sincerity of your love by comparing it with the earnestness of others. For you know the grace of our Lord Jesus Christ, that though he was rich, yet for your sakes he became poor, so that you through his poverty might become rich. 2 CORINTHIANS 8:1–9

Remember this: Whoever sows sparingly will also reap sparingly, and whoever shows generously will also reap generously. Each man should give what he has decided in his heart to give, not reluctantly or under compulsion, for God loves a cheerful giver. 2 CORINTHIANS 9:6–7

As he looked up, Jesus saw the rich putting their gifts into the temple treasury. He also saw a poor widow put in two very small copper coins. 'I tell you the truth,' he said, 'this poor widow has put in more than all the others. All these people gave their gifts out of their wealth; but she out of her poverty put in all she had to live on.' LUKE 21:1–4

The New Testament has much to say about money, particularly in the teaching of our Lord. We have a God who likes to work through earthy things – bread and wine for instance – and money is one of the things he uses to bless us, especially the money we give away. Giving money to the Lord's work can be a struggle, a duty that we grudgingly carry out. But St Paul says: *God loves a CHEERFUL giver*, and there's the difficulty. For we are not cheerful about it, and we do not want to pretend. See if St Paul can help us make our giving as cheerful and natural a part of our Christian lives as singing hymns. It seems to have been like that with the church in Macedonia.

God's self-giving

Our Lord Jesus Christ became poor so that we might share in his riches; consider the magnificent generosity with which he gave it all up for us. When we see this we may begin to express the same sort of generosity in our dealings with God and with the world. This was the grace God had given the Macedonian churches. *Extreme poverty, welling up in rich generosity*, and all *with overflowing joy*. They had become rich indeed; for look how like our Lord those Macedonian Christians had become!

Giving ourselves

They gave themselves first to the Lord, and then to us in keeping with God's will. Until we give ourselves there is something phoney about the money we put in the collection plate. It divides the part of our lives we give to the Lord from the part we hold back. Until we recognise that ALL we have is his, ALL is from him, and ALL is due to him, we are not really giving anything. But when we give ourselves to the Lord and are living it out in service to others, then everything changes. The part we put in the plate represents ALL we have and ALL we are. The giving of money, time and ability becomes the very means of giving ourselves to him.

An overflowing heart

The collection in Macedonia came from an overflowing heart, not an overflowing purse. They saw it as an opportunity for thanksgiving. Their giving said it all, like the woman in the Gospels who threw into the treasury all she had left. What a lovely act of worship! What are you saying to God by your giving?

Our God loves to give. He is a most cheerful giver. We too should love to give, with a cheerfulness that matches his – if that were possible. He always gives more than we can ever give to him. God has no debtors. When I get to heaven I long to meet that widow who gave her two last coins. 'Did you go hungry to bed that night?' I shall ask. I would like to think she had a most marvellous supper; somehow the good Lord could do it. I do not want your money. What I want is the joy and blessing that will be yours when you learn about cheerful giving. I long to see the mind and heart of Christ pulsating in your life. For that is what he means by riches.

Saturday – Lent 5

Love rejected

As he approached Jerusalem and saw the city, he wept over it and said, 'If you, even you, had only known on this day what would bring you peace – but now it is hidden from your eyes. The days will come upon you when your enemies . . . will encircle you and . . . will not leave one stone on another, because you did not recognise the time of God's coming to you.' LUKE 19:41–44

O Jerusalem, Jerusalem, you who kill the prophets and stone those sent to you, how often I have longed to gather your children together, as a hen gathers her chicks under her wings, but you were not willing! LUKE 13:34

It was a great time for the company of disciples. Now at last their Jesus was coming into his kingdom. Their enthusiasm knew no bounds. But Jesus wept as he saw the hatred and rejection that confronted him, and the awful destiny of the city that had turned against its Lord. In a few days all these shouting disciples would be scattered and disillusioned, and the Lord would drink a cup of suffering whose depths even he could not foresee.

He had tried to warn these disciples, but they would not listen – even the twelve. It is always the way with disciples – longing for Easter, and hoping to bypass Calvary. But soon their eyes would be opened. Then they would take up their cross and follow him; and there would be new believers to train in that path of discipleship. From the first they did this chiefly by re-living with them the story of that last fateful week with their Lord – HOLY WEEK.

I have for many years followed a practice during Holy Week of reading the full story of the Passion in one of the Gospels. We shall hear some of it in church. But there is special value in reading it, thoughtfully, by yourself, *at a sitting*. It does not take half an hour with any of the first three Gospels, though you might want to think about it for much longer than that.*

So join me and all the Church next week in re-living that story.

---

* Matthew 26,27; Mark 14,15; Luke 22,23; John 13,18,19

Learn again with me how awful sin is, which demands so dreadful a remedy. Ponder again how deep is the love of our God, prepared to go to such lengths. Know once more how much you matter to him. And then on Easter Day there will be nothing hollow about your discipleship.

Mingle in imagination with those fickle crowds in the streets; feel the bewilderment of those well-meaning disciples; gasp at the calculating injustice of Pilate and the brutish cruelty of the soldiers; know the horror of Simon of Cyrene forced to carry the instrument of execution. Let the unrestrained malice of the priests chill your heart; look on numbly as the soldiers play dice, and the bystanders go on their way uninvolved and indifferent. And kneel for a while to share the agony of Mary and John. You will not fail to identify the world we live in with that ever-present story. We still do these things to each other; the suffering of the world still has that nightmare quality, and the Lord Jesus still feels every pang of it. He longs still to gather his chicks under his wings.

Above all, draw near and identify with the central character of the story. Move with Jesus along his path of sorrow. It is not really hard to share his feelings, for they are not complicated, just plain good. Only at the final step must you draw back; human imagination cannot fathom what it meant to bear the sin of the whole world. We may not know and cannot tell what that ultimate horror of evil was like. He went to that place so that we might never have to, and you must step aside as he enters.

But as you do so, do not forget to leave with him all those burdens of your life that you find intolerable: your sin of course, with your selfishness, apathy and weakness of love. Leave there the injuries you have received and the unfairness of life's lot, your bitterness, resentment and sorrow, and your remorse over lost opportunities. Leave behind the showy 'good' deeds that boost your self-image; the times when you were indifferent when you should have cared deeply; the times when you were 'right' but without love; the battles you won but thereby wounded your brother. Willingly the good Lord bears it all away into the darkness; and will crucify it for ever. It was all done for you at Calvary. I would like to share this experience of Holy Week with you all. Then we shall enter together into the holy calm of Easter Eve – a peace that passes understanding – and the radiant certainty of Easter Day and Pentecost.

O Jesus, Master Carpenter of Nazareth, who on the cross through wood and nails worked Man's whole salvation: wield well your tools in this your workshop; that we who come to you rough-hewn may by your hand be fashioned to a truer beauty and a greater usefulness; for the honour of your holy name.

C.I.T.C. Schools Prayer, Nairobi
20th Century

Discussion Starters – *5th Week in Lent*

1. Can the will of God really be more important to us than following our own personal satisfaction and fulfilment?

2. Taking up our cross and following Christ may well be tough; but Mother Julian asserted: *All shall be well*. Was she being realistic?

3. Our giving of time, money and talents is meant to express our commitment and love for the Lord. How can we prevent it becoming just a rule of life reluctantly taken on board?

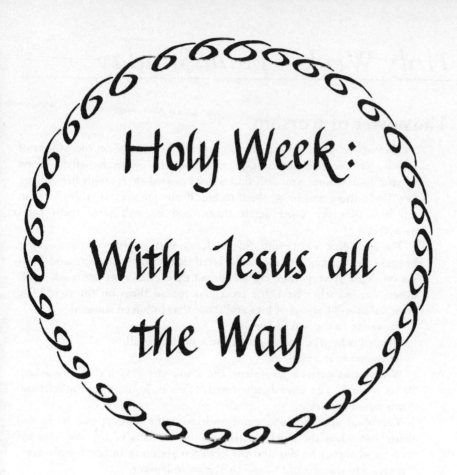

Holy Week: With Jesus all the Way

THE FULFILMENT OF LOVE

Thanks be to you, Lord Jesus Christ, for all the benefits you have given us, for all the pains and insults you have borne for us. Most merciful Redeemer, Friend, and Brother, may we know you more clearly, love you more dearly, and follow you more nearly, now and for evermore.

St Richard of Chichester
13th Century

Holy Week – Palm Sunday

The power of worship

> As they approached Jerusalem and came to Bethphage on the Mount of Olives, Jesus sent two disciples, saying to them, 'Go to the village ahead of you, and at once you will find a donkey tied there, with her colt by her. Untie them and bring them to me. If anyone says anything to you, tell him that the Lord needs them, and he will send them right away.' . . .
>
> The disciples went and did as Jesus had instructed them. They brought the donkey and the colt, placed their cloaks on them, and Jesus sat on them. A very large crowd spread their cloaks on the road, while others cut branches from the trees and spread them on the road. The crowd that went ahead of him and those that followed shouted,
>
> 'Hosanna to the Son of David!'
>
> 'Blessed is he who comes in the name of the Lord!'
>
> 'Hosanna in the highest!'
>
> When Jesus entered Jerusalem, the whole city was stirred and asked, 'Who is this?' The crowds answered, 'This is Jesus, the prophet from Nazareth in Galilee'. . . .
>
> The blind and the lame came to him at the temple, and he healed them. But when the chief priests and the teachers of the law saw the wonderful things he did and the children shouting in the temple area, 'Hosanna to the Son of David,' they were indignant.
>
> 'Do you hear what these children are saying?' they asked him.
>
> 'Yes,' replied Jesus, 'have you never read, "From the lips of children and infants you have ordained praise?"'   MATTHEW 21:1–16

It was a time for extravagant gestures – a time when anything else would have been mean and calculating. There was the man who proudly lent Jesus his donkey. You might well object if you found your car being borrowed by a smiling stranger. But if he told you it was needed by the Queen that would be different; and you would be telling your friends about it for the rest of your life. So it must have been with that man. 'Jesus used MY donkey. This is the very animal he sat on', with an affectionate slap on its side. An extravagant gesture perhaps, but I am sure he never regretted it.

There were the people who spread their cloaks on the road in front of him. It reminds us of Sir Walter Raleigh spreading his cloak over a puddle for Queen Elizabeth I. For that royal person he was proud to do it. But this procession into Jerusalem was bearing a greater than Queen Elizabeth I or II. Did those people regret ruining their cloaks? Of course not! 'This is the cloak that Jesus rode over that day,' they would proudly tell their grandchildren. 'Look at the mud stains; and this is the hole where the donkey's hoof ripped it on a stone.'

The power of true worship

There were those who cut down branches from the trees to wave like banners. What an extraordinary thing to do! But not that day. Anything else would have been less than human. It needed that sort of gesture to unlock the joy and praise that welled up in every heart. As they gave themselves wholeheartedly to praise and worship the conviction grew in their hearts that every word they uttered was wonderfully true. Here indeed was he who came in the name of the Lord. *Hosanna in the highest!*

Do not be afraid of real worship, even when it goes a bit over the top! The form of worship depends on the culture in which it arises. But always heartfelt worship unlocks faith. Praise deepens assurance. Thanksgiving creates certainty.

All that week Jesus was surrounded by extravagant gestures: there was the poor widow who put all she had to live on into the collection box (Mark 12:41–44); and there was the woman who broke a whole bottle of perfume over his feet (Mark 14:3–9). Why did they do it? Can you understand? I hope you can. For disciples who know how to worship like that have learnt how to give their hearts to the One who gave so much for them. That at least the crowds got right.

Holy week – Monday

Keep watch with me

> Then Jesus went with his disciples to a place called Gethsemane, and he said to them, 'Sit here while I go over there and pray.' He took Peter and the two sons of Zebedee along with him, and he began to be sorrowful and troubled. Then he said to them, 'My soul is overwhelmed with sorrow to the point of death. Stay here and keep watch with me.'
>
> Going a little farther, he fell with his face to the ground and prayed, 'My Father, if it is possible, may this cup be taken from me. Yet not as I will, but as you will.'
>
> Then he returned to his disciples and found them sleeping. 'Could you men not keep watch with me for one hour?' he asked Peter. 'Watch and pray so that you will not fall into temptation. The spirit is willing, but the body is weak.'
>
> He went away a second time and prayed, 'My Father, if it is not possible for this cup to be taken away unless I drink it, may your will be done.' When he came back, he again found them sleeping, because their eyes were heavy. So he left them and went away once more and prayed the third time, saying the same thing.
>
> Then he returned to the disciples and said to them, 'Are you still sleeping and resting? Look the hour is near, and the Son of Man is betrayed into the hands of sinners. Rise, let us go! Here comes my betrayer!'   MATTHEW 26:36–46

As Jesus entered the garden he left behind at the entrance eight of the disciples, and went on with his most intimate group, Peter, James and John. Then he told even them to stop, while he moved to the lonely prayer that only the Saviour of the world could utter.

A lonely battle

The work of winning our salvation was something that Jesus alone could do. The Church plays no part in it; Jesus bore the whole weight of our sin alone, and it nearly crushed him. We can never add in the smallest way to the great sacrifice of our Lord Jesus Christ. No prayer or fasting of ours, no act of dedication or sacrifice on our part will affect it in the least. Jesus at the lowest point of human weakness proved stronger than all the powers of evil, and worked our whole salvation by himself. All we can do is look on in amazement, and worship and place our trust in him.

For love of a friend
We cannot help in this work, but our Lord yearned for human fellowship as he undertook it. From Peter and the others he did not get it, though John later came to the foot of the cross to join the two Mary's there. He asks us now in the 20th Century to watch with him, at this season when the attention of his Church is turned towards his Cross and Passion. We do this, not in order to achieve anything, but because our Lord Jesus values the warmth of our companionship, though to watch with him is also a definite protection against temptation, as he told the slumbering Peter – soon to fall so badly. But we do it for his sake and for the joy of being close to him.

We need to examine our motives sternly at this point. If we have little desire to be with him and to watch with him, then we do well to admit it and confess it with sorrow. Christians have always seen it as a holy obligation of love to watch with our Lord during Holy Week and especially on Good Friday.

The only way
We should ponder the prayer of Jesus: *My Father, IF IT IS POSSIBLE, may this cup be taken from me.* That prayer was heard; the answer was NO. Even divine omnipotence could find no other way. It is only through the cross of Jesus that we may be saved. I repeat, we are saved through the cross of Jesus or not at all.

When the Lord returned to his lonely vigil the second and third times, the prayer is subtly changed: *My Father, if it is NOT possible for this cup to be taken away UNLESS I DRINK IT, may your will be done.* He must drink the cup of suffering for sin so that we may be spared that awful fate. Because he loves us he will take the deadly draft and drain it to the dregs to set us free. After that prayer all hesitation vanishes, and Jesus marches out full of divine assurance on the path that leads down to the darkest place in the universe. We shall join him in death when our time comes. But he will be there to meet us and all will be light. The outer darkness, the place of total separation, we need never even look at; for he endured it in our place in the dark hours on the cross.

Holy week – Tuesday

How to handle injustice

Then the men stepped forward, seized Jesus and arrested him. With that, one of Jesus' companions reached for his sword, drew it out and struck the servant of the high priest, cutting off his ear.

'Put your sword back in its place,' Jesus said to him, 'for all who draw the sword will die by the sword. Do you think I cannot call on my Father, and he will at once put at my disposal more than twelve legions of angels? . . . Then all the disciples deserted him and fled.

Those who had arrested Jesus took him to Caiaphas, the high priest, where the teachers of the law and the elders had assembled. But Peter followed him at a distance. . . .

The chief priests and the whole Sanhedrin were looking for false evidence against Jesus so that they could put him to death. But they did not find any, though many false witnesses came forward. . . . The the high priest stood up and said to Jesus, 'Are you not going to answer? What is this testimony that these men are bringing against you?' But Jesus remained silent. The high priest said to him, 'I charge you under oath by the living God: Tell us if you are the Christ, the Son of God.'

'Yes, it is as you say,' Jesus replied. 'But I say to all of you: In future you will see the Son of Man sitting at the right hand of the Mighty One and coming on the clouds of heaven.'

Then the high priest tore his clothes and said, 'He has spoken blasphemy! Why do we need any more witnesses? Look, now you have heard the blasphemy. What do you think?'

'He is worthy of death,' they answered. Then they spat in his face and struck him with their fists. . . .

Now Peter was sitting out in the courtyard, and a servant girl came to him. 'You also were with Jesus of Galilee,' she said. But he denied it before them all. 'I don't know what you're talking about,' he said. Then he went out to the gateway, where another girl saw him and said to the people there, 'This fellow was with Jesus of Nazareth.' He denied it again, with an oath: 'I don't know the man!'

After a little while, those standing there went up to Peter and said, 'Surely you are one of them, for your accent gives you away.' Then he began to call down curses on himself and he swore to them, 'I don't know the man!' Immediately a cock crowed. Then Peter remembered the word Jesus had spoken: 'Before the cock crows, you will disown me three times.' And he went outside and wept bitterly.

Early in the morning, all the chief priests and the elders of the people came to the decision to put Jesus to death. They bound him, led him away and turned him over to Pilate, the governor.

MATTHEW 26:50–75; 27:1–2

It is significant that our Lord was crucified for being what he was. Before the high priest he was condemned for being *the Christ, the Son of God*; and before Pilate for being *the King of the Jews* – true again, though not in the way they meant. This was the charge nailed above the cross. Try as they might, the only charge that would stick, even in the hands of that unscrupulous bunch, was the truth.

The whole procedure was illegal; the Sanhedrin was forbidden to meet at night; and the only evidence was the word of the prisoner himself, which was not heard by the formal daylight sitting of the court at first light. But Caiaphas needed to get the prisoner tried, executed and buried before the start of the special Sabbath at sundown. So legality and justice were swept aside. It is an all too familiar story in our world – how the unscrupulous triumph.

Non-resistance
The disciples were not prepared for it. Peter was spoiling for a fight! Probably they would have died to a man. But this confident non-resistance was too much. They just did not understand. Peter eventually learnt his lesson well: *If you suffer for doing good and you endure it, this is commendable before God. To this you were called, because Christ suffered for you, leaving you an example, that you should follow in his steps.* (1 Peter 2:20–23)

Be an open Christian
The hardest temptation for many young Christians is to deny that they belong to Christ; the challenge usually comes from brash unbelieving friends. It is a sad byway to enter, as Peter found. (There is, of course, a way back, as Peter's story later showed.) But better settle it now in your mind what you are going to say. 'Yes, I'm a Christian,' is a straightforward statement that usually earns respect. It may be that your friends *need* your firm witness.

Holy week – Wednesday

The point of decision

Pilate called together the chief priests, the rulers and the people, and said to them, 'You brought me this man as one who was inciting the people to rebellion. I have examined him in your presence and have found no basis for your charges against him. . . . He has done nothing to deserve death. Therefore, I will punish him and then release him.'

With one voice they cried out, 'Away with this man! Release Barabbas to us!' (Barabbas had been thrown into prison for an insurrection in the city, and for murder.)

Wanting to release Jesus, Pilate appealed to them again. But they kept shouting, 'Crucify him! Crucify him!'

For the third time he spoke to them: 'Why? What crime has this man committed? I have found in him no grounds for the death penalty. Therefore I will have him punished and then release him.'

But with loud shouts they insistently demanded that he be crucified, and their shouts prevailed. So Pilate decided to grant their demand. . . . and surrendered Jesus to their will.

As they led him away, they seized Simon from Cyrene, who was on his way in from the country, and put the cross on him and made him carry it behind Jesus. . . .

Two other men, both criminals, were also led out with him to be executed. When they came to the place called *The Skull*, there they crucified him, along with the criminals – one on his right, the other on his left. Jesus said, 'Father, forgive them, for they do not know what they are doing.' . . .

There was a written notice above him, which read:

THIS IS THE KING OF THE JEWS.

One of the criminals who hung there hurled insults at him: 'Aren't you the Christ? Save yourself and us!'

But the other criminal rebuked him. 'Don't you fear God,' he said, 'since you are under the same sentence? We are punished justly, for we are getting what our deeds deserve. But this man has done nothing wrong.'

Then he said, 'Jesus, remember me when you come into your kingdom.'

Jesus answered him, 'I tell you the truth, today you will be with me in paradise.' LUKE 23:13–43.

Observe closely how our Lord dealt with people that day.

Silence before deliberate sin
Pilate had only contempt for these people he ruled; but they were a rung on his career ladder, and he needed a good report from them. One innocent Jew could be sacrificed for that. The chief priests were envious of Jesus' influence, and needed him out of the way. The crowd resented the foreign occupying power, and admired the terrorist Barabbas, who had slit a few Roman throats. This Jesus would have them all loving their enemies if they gave him a chance. Our Lord remains silent. He has nothing to say to deliberate sin, unless we turn from it.

Compassion before ignorance
There were many caught up in that day's events by accident. They never meant to be involved, and did not understand what was going on – the soldiers obeying orders, and the crowds along the way. For these our Lord has only compassion: *Father, forgive them, for they do not know what they are doing.* God alone knows how many people down the centuries have been covered by that prayer; countless millions, I guess.

Poor Simon of Cyrene, *forced* to help! But I imagine the thank-you he received made him feel it a real privilege. He may well have become a Christian; Mark's Gospel refers to him as *the father of Alexander and Rufus* (Mark 15:21). You know, Mark says, Rufus and Alexander's dad – as though the family was well-known in the Church.

Release for the penitent
Look at the change of heart of that hardened criminal as he turns to Jesus. Suddenly he has a real sense of sin and of its just reward; and he feels a real concern for his fellow criminal. Astonishingly, he sees in this battered man dying beside him his Saviour. The work of grace in the human heart is truly amazing. If our Lord Jesus Christ can find such a one as this in his last moments, there can be none of us beyond his reach.

Our Lord hangs between the angry and the penitent, and will bring them both release – if only they turn to him. But only one does. If some are saved in the hour of death, others are not. It is sad, but we Christians must be realists.

Holy week – Maundy Thursday

The eternal meal

> And he took bread, gave thanks and broke it, and gave it to them, saying, 'This is my body given for you; do this in remembrance of me.' In the same way, after supper he took the cup, saying, 'This cup is the new covenant in my blood, which is poured out for you.'   LUKE 22:19–21

> After Jesus said this, he looked towards heaven and prayed: 'Father, the time has come. Glorify your Son, that your Son may glorify you. For you granted him authority over all people that he might give eternal life to all those you have given him. Now this is eternal life: that they may know you, the only true God, and Jesus Christ, whom you have sent. I have brought you glory on earth by completing the work you gave me to do. And now, Father, glorify me in your presence with the glory I had with you before the world began. I have revealed you to those whom you gave me out of the world. They were yours; you gave them to me and they have obeyed your word. . . .
>
> 'My prayer is not for them alone. I pray also for those who will believe in me through their message, that all of them may be one, Father, just as you are in me and I am in you. May they also be in us so that the world may believe that you have sent me. . . .
>
> 'Father, I want those you have given me to be with me where I am, and to see my glory, the glory you have given me because you loved me before the creation of the world.'   JOHN 17:1–6; 20–24

There is a sense in which there has only ever been ONE Holy Communion service. It started long ago in that upper room with our Lord and the Twelve. It continues wherever the Church meets to break bread in remembrance of him – in houses, catacombs and churches, in abbeys and cathedrals, by sick-beds and in hospitals – wherever the Church gathers to share in the eternal celebration feast of its Lord. It binds together Christians of all races and cultures. We renew our assurance of belonging to him and to each other; we know again his promised presence, and are nourished by his life.

Re-adjust the focus of your mind, and look afresh at that upper room. In the centre is our Lord, surrounded by the close circle of the Twelve. Around them are other figures we know from the gospel stories. Further back in the shadows (but the walls are no longer there) are Christians from every corner of the world – saints, martyrs, bishops, missionaries, and many many others who lived out holy lives to pass on to us the good news of the Gospel – and the attention of them all is only for Jesus. Beyond them rank upon rank, tier upon tier, *a multitude that no-one could count, from every nation, tribe, people and language* (Revelation 7:9), filling everything, it seems, to the bounds of the galaxy. Yet each one is also close to that central group and near, very near, to the Lord. And still the bread is broken and the wine poured out, and passed out to his disciples.

I am not asking you just to make an effort of the imagination, but to recognise a spiritual reality – *The Communion of Saints*, the Creed calls it. For that great fellowship meal is an eternal event that continues in Heaven: *For the wedding supper of the Lamb has come, and his bride has made herself ready. Then the angel said to me, 'Write: "Blessed are those who are invited to the wedding supper of the Lamb!"'* (Revelation 19:7–9)

We share that Supper now with those in the glory of heaven – *with angels and archangels and with all the company of heaven*, as the time-honoured phrase has it. Those we have loved and lost are there too – with us at the Table, at the far end where the light is too bright for us to see. Our Lord Jesus still joins us and them; for he is the one tangible link between Earth and Heaven.

Our Lord Jesus is the **Host** at this meal; and he has issued a personal invitation to each and every one of us. There is a place for you at his Table, and there always will be. Even Judas was not excluded – if only he had come back!

Our Lord Jesus is the **Victim** in this sacrificial feast, *the Lamb of God who takes away the sin of the world* (John 1:29), who *by one sacrifice has made perfect for ever those who are being made holy.* (Hebrews 10:14)

Our Lord Jesus is the **Food** of his people, who nourishes our souls, and says, *I am the bread of life.* (John 6:48) Eternal life is a new quality of life, that starts now and goes on for ever. It is a life that consists in *knowing the only true God, and Jesus Christ, whom he has sent.* It is a life we share in an all-embracing fellowship with his people everywhere.

Together at the Cross

> Pilate had a notice prepared and fastened to the cross. It read, JESUS OF NAZARETH, THE KING OF THE JEWS. Many of the Jews read this sign, for the place ... was near the city, ... The chief priests of the Jews protested to Pilate, 'Do not write "The King of the Jews," but that this man claimed to be king of the Jews.' Pilate answered, 'What I have written, I have written'. ...
>
> Near the cross of Jesus stood his mother, his mother's sister, Mary the wife of Clopas, and Mary of Magdala. When Jesus saw his mother there, and the disciple whom he loved standing near by, he said to his mother, 'Dear woman, here is your son,' and to the disciple, 'Here is your mother.' From that time on, this disciple took her into his home.
>
> Later, knowing that all was now completed, and so that the Scripture would be fulfilled, Jesus said, 'I am thirsty.' A jar of wine vinegar was there, so they soaked a sponge in it, put the sponge on a stalk of the hyssop plant, and lifted it to Jesus' lips. When he had received the drink, Jesus said, 'It is finished.' With that, he bowed his head and gave up his spirit. JOHN 19:19–30

So we take our place beside the cross. We close our ears to the spite of the chief priests, humiliated by Pilate over the inscription – unwittingly Pilate got it right, we notice. We walk past the soldiers, gambling for their perks. And we take our place with the Church gathered there at the foot of the cross.

They were numb, unable to take it in – held in a waking nightmare with no release. Not only were they losing a son, a nephew, a quite special friend; they were losing their God! They had seen in Jesus the one who came from the Father, full of grace and truth. They had rebuilt their lives around him, and now this ...

The three Mary's and John, each suffering, each alone, and separate in their loss; people usually are in bereavement. The Mother of Jesus, unique in all the human race – was this what it meant to be highly favoured by God, to have such a sword as this piercing her soul? Her sister there beside her, loyal, helpful – but how could she share the wilderness in Mary's soul? Mary Magdalen, emotional, effusive, rescued by Jesus from a life of depravity – how could she relate to the tortured calm of his mother? Her way was different. John, the beloved disciple – not for nothing had the Lord nick-named him *Son of Thunder*. Only recently he had wanted to call down fire from heaven on a village that turned them away. John, the angry young man, slowly being loved by Jesus into true discipleship.

Then, with a handful of words and a painful movement of the head, our Lord re-adjusts the tensions and brings his own together once more. With mother and disciple at one, the others would be able to join them. Bereavement need not be an isolating experience for Christians. In the darkness the love of Jesus bonds us together.

But there is a parable in our Lord's action that we must not miss. Indeed it is a sacramental moment. Here Mother Church is bidden to accept as her own that awkward, angular disciple – perhaps a new convert recently come to the Lord; he is bursting with too much enthusiasm, and often acts foolishly. The Church backs away from such a one. No! *Here is your son*, says the Lord.

Likewise, that disciple must accept his Mother, the Church, and it is not easy. She seems to him more an obstacle than a help. Her wrinkles and faults and stuffy old ways are hard to put up with! But for the Lord's sake Mother Church is to be received, respected and loved by every son and daughter the Lord calls.

John needs Mary's faith and she needs his youth and his close insight into the heart of his Lord and friend. Together they would ensure that her children down the years would be many, and the true knowledge of the Lord would be carried everywhere.

Now darkness descends on the scene; the Father draws a veil over that which Man may not see. There in the silence God in Christ draws into his own being the ultimate penalty for the sin of the world, and bears it alone, and bears it away. *My God, my God, why have you forsaken me?* (Matthew 27:45–46) What is this? God forsaken by God? Do not ask too many questions. The outer darkness, the place without God, is the inevitable end of sin. The Lord once pictured that place in a parable: *Have pity on me and send Lazarus to dip the tip of his finger in water and cool my tongue, because I am in agony in this fire.* (Luke 16:24) We hear just one utterance now to illuminate his feelings: *I am thirsty.* It speaks volumes.

Meekly Jesus bows his head, and surrenders his spirit.

Holy week – Saturday

It is finished

> The soldiers therefore came and broke the legs of the first man who had
> been crucified with Jesus, and then those of the other. But when they
> came to Jesus and found that he was already dead, they did not break
> his legs. Instead, one of the soldiers pierced Jesus' side with a spear,
> bringing a sudden flow of blood and water. the man who saw it has
> given testimony, and his testimony is true. He knows that he tells the
> truth, and he testifies so that you also may believe.
>
> Later, Joseph of Arimathea asked Pilate for the body of Jesus. Now
> Joseph was a disciple of Jesus, but secretly because he feared the Jews.
> With Pilate's permission, he came and took the body. He was ac-
> companied by Nicodemus, the man who earlier had visited Jesus at
> night. Nicodemus brought a mixture of myrrh and aloes, about seventy-
> five pounds. Taking Jesus' body, the two of them wrapped it, with the
> spices, in strips of linen. This was in accordance with Jewish burial
> customs. At the place where Jesus was crucified, there was a garden,
> and in the garden a new tomb, in which no-one had ever been laid.
> Because it was the Jewish day of Preparation and since the tomb was
> near by, they laid Jesus there.   JOHN 19:32–35 & 38–42

The final word from the cross is a cry of fulfilment. In English the
word *finished* could imply resignation to fate: 'It's all over. This is the
end. I've had it.' But the Greek word carries no such sense. It is rather
the word an artist or craftsman might use as he puts the finishing
touch to his masterpiece. It is a word used again and again in the
Gospels; each time Matthew comes to the end of one of the great
teaching sessions of Jesus – the Sermon on the Mount, the great
parables about the Kingdom, and so on (Matthew 7:28, 13:53) – he
uses this word: *When Jesus had* FINISHED *saying these things* . . . There
was nothing more to be said; divine wisdom had spoken the last word.

Thus it was at the end of our Lord's Passion: Jesus, *knowing that
all was now completed* (same word), *and so that the Scripture would
be fulfilled* (closely related word), *said* . . . The last sorrow had been
borne, the last penalty for sin had been paid, the final weight of evil
had been endured; obedience to the will of the Father had been fully
lived out. The dark cloud that hid the face of God from Man had been

lifted. The perfect offering of Man to God had been made. There was nothing left to do, and our Lord surrendered his life into his Father's hands.

The receding tide
Isaiah's prophetic poem uses an ancient image to express this:

> *'To me this is like the days of Noah,*
> *when I swore that the waters of Noah*
> *would never again cover the earth.*
> *So now I have sworn not to be angry with you,*
> *never to rebuke you again.*
> *Though the mountains be shaken and the hills be removed,*
> *yet my unfailing love for you will not be shaken*
> *nor my covenant of peace be removed,'*
> *says the Lord, who has compassion on you.* Isaiah 54:9–10

We are reminded of the way a receding tide leaves the beach smooth and clear, with all the footprints and marks of yesterday erased and forgotten. The waters of Noah, when they receded, left a world cleansed of evil and ready for a new start.

So when the life of Jesus receded there was a world cleansed, open to God as it had never been before, and ready for a fresh start. The cleansing flood released from his side by the spear-thrust was a great symbolic expression of this, falling to earth to cleanse and refresh. Every detail was etched on St John's memory, and he tells it to us so that we might see and believe.

Open disciples at last
At last Joseph of Arimathea and Nicodemus found the courage to come into the open and admit they were disciples of Jesus. It was probably the biggest spiritual battle of their lives. It is so for many people. Those who try and keep their faith entirely private are always rather sad Christians, never very sure of anything. But at last all that is changed. They know where they stand, and so does the rest of the world; and there is strength in that position. Being part of his Church openly and unashamedly is an essential part of our salvation. As St Paul put it: *It is with your heart that you believe and are justified, and it is with your mouth that you confess and are saved.* (Romans 10:10) May the Lord give you great joy as you join with his people at this blessed season.

Assist us mercifully with your help, O Lord God of our salvation, that we may enter with joy upon the meditation of those mighty acts whereby you have given us life and immortality; through Jesus Christ our Lord.

The American Prayer Book
18th Century

Discussion Starters – *Holy Week*

1. Our Lord's response to the evil of injustice was no mere submission. Trace the way he deals with Caiaphas, Pilate, and the soldiers, and the example of divine love in action he gives us.

2. Ponder the downward path poor Peter took on the night of Christ's betrayal – his brash self-confidence, his sleeping, his aggression, his following at a distance, and then his repeated failure when challenged. What lessons and warnings can we draw for ourselves from this?

3. How far is it right for Christians to be a bit triumphalist in their worship? When is it right to assert the inevitable final triumph of our God and his Christ; and when should we be quiet and grieve beside a world that suffers? Consider the example of Jesus.

Easter Day: Witnesses of these things

WITH US TO THE END OF THE AGE

O God, who through the mighty resurrection of your Son
Jesus Christ delivered us from the power of darkness and
brought us into the kingdom of your love: grant that as he
was raised from the dead by the glory of the Father, so we
also may walk in newness of life and seek those things that
are above, where with you, O Father, and the Holy Spirit,
he lives and reigns for ever and ever.

The Gelasian Sacramentary
5th Century

Easter Sunday

A new hope

The angel said to the women, 'Do not be afraid, for I know that you are looking for Jesus, who was crucified. He is not here; he has risen, just as he said. Come and see the place where he lay. Then go quickly and tell his disciples: "He has risen from the dead and is going ahead of you into Galilee. There you will see him." Now I have told you.'

MATTHEW 28:5–7

Jesus himself stood among them and said to them, 'Peace be with you.' They were startled and frightened, thinking they saw a ghost. He said to them, 'Why are you troubled, and why do doubts rise in your minds? Look at my hands and my feet. It is I myself! Touch me and see; a ghost does not have flesh and bones, as you see I have.'

When he had said this, he showed them his hands and feet. And while they still did not believe it because of joy and amazement, he asked them, 'Do you have anything here to eat?' They gave him a piece of broiled fish, and he took it and ate it in their presence.   LUKE 24:36–43

They would see him in Galilee, was the message of the angels. In point of fact they did see him, several times, in Jerusalem; but what mattered was meeting him in Galilee, their own familiar stamping ground, the setting where they normally lived their lives. Jerusalem was special; it was the HOLY city. It was in Galilee that they must find him. And this is the message for us: YOU must meet Jesus for yourself, in YOUR Galilee, where he will be real to YOU.

Touching him

The Lord invites his disciples to *touch* him; and he invites us also to reach out and discover in our experience that he is real. The Apostles could do it by putting out their hands. That is not for us. But if Jesus Christ is the Son of God, we must experience him in the same way people always experience God – by an inner knowledge that is hard to describe, but is as definite as life itself. Our difficulty is in accepting that spiritual things are just as real as physical things – indeed more real, because they are permanent.

The evidence

But we have minds as well as spirits; so let us look at the evidence carefully and scientifically. First, we are dealing with an unrepeatable event. Has Science therefore nothing to say about it? Oh yes! Many a past event is unique in recorded history. The great meteorite that hit Siberia in 1908 was of this sort. But Science can study it. The meteorite left its mark and we may look at that, even many years later; and there are reports of eye witnesses that may be tested and compared. So let us approach the Resurrection of Jesus Christ in these ways.

The obvious mark left on the world is the Church. You may not think much of the Church! But how did it come into existence? Did a bunch of frightened, poorly educated Jews dream up a myth about a risen Christ and foist it on the world? Clearly those men believed it; and their message of a crucified and risen Lord proved to be strangely compelling, sweeping through one community after another. Could such men deliberately proclaim what they knew to be a lie? All this you can study and think about in the 20th Century.

The testimony

They insisted that their encounters with the risen Christ were physical: no body left in the tomb; grave clothes neatly folded up, and so on. They could touch Jesus. He broke a loaf of bread. He ate fish. He lit a fire and cooked breakfast on it. But they also knew he had been present when they did not see him. He knew what they had been talking about, and was aware of their thoughts without having to be told. At the end of 40 days those disciples were completely convinced of the reality of the risen Christ.

Since then countless other sane, balanced people have claimed to share this experience, mostly without setting eyes on the risen Christ. If you have journeyed thus far with me through Lent, YOU must know he is alive and with you too. He may have called into question many of your attitudes and ways. But you have responded because you want to live your life in the REAL world; and if Jesus is real, he is the most important part of reality. Your assurance will grow as you continue to follow him. Your faith may receive many knocks and trials – just like the Apostles – but this assurance will protect you, and your testimony will ring as true as theirs, as long as you continue to walk in obedience.

Epilogue

A new commission

> On the evening of that first day of the week, when the disciples were together, with the doors locked for fear of the Jews, Jesus came and stood among them and said, 'Peace be with you!' After he said this, he showed them his hands and side. The disciples were overjoyed when they saw the Lord.
>
> Again Jesus said, 'Peace be with you! As the Father has sent me, I am sending you.' And with that he breathed on them and said, 'Receive the Holy Spirit. If you forgive anyone his sins, they are forgiven; if you do not forgive them, they are not forgiven.' JOHN 20:19–23

The most important thing about the Resurrection of Jesus Christ is that it happened. But what then? What effect should it have in our lives? What difference should it make in our community?

Reconciliation

They were startled and frightened by the unexpected and the unknown, as anyone might be. But they also had every reason to feel ill-at-ease in the Lord's presence. They had let him down badly; they had deserted him, denied him, and behaved like frightened rabbits. Yet the Lord's first thought is to assure them of restoration; and he makes clear that the basis of this is his wounds. The Lord Jesus wants us all to know that the barrier between us and God caused by our sin has been removed by his death for us; he has borne the whole weight of our sin, so that we can be at peace in the presence of a holy God. The most important effect of the Resurrection is reconciliation with God.

The Lord's greeting also expects peace to be WITH them; he demands forgiveness, restoration and reconciliation as the prevailing attitudes among his disciples. All recrimination and fault-finding he permanently outlaws.

The Lord's own commission

As the Father has sent me, so I am sending you, the Lord says. *God who reconciled us to himself through Christ has given us the ministry of reconciliation.* (2 Corinthians 5:18–20) Thus our commission is modelled on that of Jesus. We must therefore respond obediently in

116

the same manner as Jesus, and follow the same methods of self-sacrifice and never-failing love.

The Lord Jesus knew that in seeing and hearing him, the world was seeing and hearing the Father. *When a man believes in me, he does not believe in me only, but in the one who sent me. When he looks at me, he sees the one who sent me.* (John 12:44–45) *These words you hear are not my own; they belong to the Father who sent me.* (John 14:24) Likewise, we are to live believing that Jesus is at work among us and within us. When people meet us they meet Jesus; when they hear us they hear Jesus; when they come into our fellowship they find the love of Jesus.

A new power

The Lord Jesus knows that to represent him like this in the world is a task quite beyond our unaided effort. We cannot 'turn on Jesus' by an effort of will; and if we tried to, it would be a hypocritical thing that would carry no conviction. Only the inner transforming power of the Holy Spirit can do that. So this is what the Lord bequeaths to us: *He breathed on them and said, 'Receive the Holy Spirit.'*

The gift was given, though they were not set free to use the gift of the Holy Spirit until his outpouring on the day of Pentecost seven weeks later. God often works like that. He gives us the gift of the Holy Spirit through baptism and confirmation, but we still need to find grace to release his power in our lives. And the purpose of the gift is that we should live the life of Jesus and do his work – a ministry of forgiveness, restoration and healing.

There is a whole world to be healed. Nearly two thousand years of Christianity and still so much to do! How can we believe that God's programme is realistic and will ever be fulfilled? How can we place our faith in a God who works so slowly? How commit our lives to him? There is just one sign he gives us, just one proof that he allows: JESUS ROSE FROM THE DEAD. It ought to be enough.

> To God the Father, who first loved us, and made us accepted in the Beloved; to God the Son, who loved us, and washed us from our sins in his own blood; to God the Holy Spirit, who sheds the love of God abroad in our hearts; to the one true God be all love and all glory, for time and for eternity.
>
> *Bishop Thomas Ken*
> *18th Century*